The Business Corporation
and Productive Justice

ABINGDON PRESS STUDIES IN CHRISTIAN ETHICS
AND ECONOMIC LIFE, VOLUME 3

The Business Corporation and Productive Justice

David A. Krueger

With Critical Responses by
Donald W. Shriver, Jr.
and
Laura L. Nash

Introduction by
Max L. Stackhouse

Abingdon Press
Nashville

Library of Congress Cataloging-in-Publication Data

Krueger, David A.
    The business corporation and productive justice / David A. Krueger; with critical responses by Donald W. Shriver, Jr. and Laura L. Nash; introduction by Max L. Stackhouse.
        p.   cm. — (Abingdon Press studies in Christian ethics and economic life: vol. 3)
    Includes bibliographic references.
    ISBN 0-687-02098-0 (alk. paper)
    1. Corporations—Religious aspects—Christianity. 2. Corporations—Moral and ethical aspects. 3. Capitalism—Religious aspects—Christianity. 4. Capitalism—Moral and ethical aspects. 5. Christian ethics. I. Shriver, Donald W. II. Nash, Laura L. III. Title. IV. Series: Abingdon Press studies in Christian ethics and economic life; #3.
BR115.C3K78   1997
261.8'5—dc21   97-12139
                                               CIP

Contents

Preface

This series is written to aid in the reconstruction of Christian Ethics as it bears on economic life in our increasingly global era. Reconstruction is necessary because much of the analysis used by theologians and pastors to think about economic life in the past few decades is socially and theologically suspect.

It is not only political scientists who failed to predict the collapse of Eastern Europe by failing to read the signs of the times. Nor was it only economists who argued for massive loans by private banks to doubtful governments and did not foresee the consequences of these debts. Nor can we say it was only sociologists who denied the evidence of religious resurgence around the world because they believed that modernization would secularize everyone, or only anthropologists who argued that religion is an aspect of culture and every culture's ethic is equal to every other one, or only politicians who began to see all issues only in terms of power analysis. It was not only philosophers and literary critics who began to deconstruct every normative claim. These all contributed to the demoralization of intellectual and religious life, to a vacuity in social ethics; but, it must be said, it was also the theologians and pastors.

In conferences on the implications of the Fall of the Wall sponsored by the Lilly Endowment, one hosted by Trotz Rendtorff in Munich and another by Peter Berger in Boston, it became clear that ideological differences had obscured for many the deeper social and ethical forces that shape modern life, as well as many biblical and theological motifs that are decisive for faith and ethics. It is not that no contribution to the future was made in these decades. Some evil was undone; some good was done. Many colonial, racist, and sexist structures were challenged, if not fully banished, and many people were exposed to new possibilities. But many views of what brought these about, and many of the social and theological theories that various advocates of liberation use to guide the present toward the future are thin, false, confused, or perilous. They cannot help us help us discover the ethical fabric necessary for a global society, or the theological bases by which to discern or construct one.

We are closer to Ezra and Nehemiah (rebuilding the city on the base of the past) or the early church (engaging and reshaping a cosmopolitan culture) than we are to the Exodus, the Conquest, the Apocalypse, or the New Jerusalem. The prophetic task today is to reconstruct social ethics boldly, under insecure and ambiguous conditions, while confessing our sins and seeking to be socially realistic, intellectually cogent, and theologically faithful.

To reform ethics, we offer a series of volumes, exploring the following hypotheses, recognizing that not everyone agrees:

- We face the prospect of a worldwide, multicultural society in which democratic constitutional polities, human rights, ethnic interests, nationalist forces, media images, and corporate capitalist forces will be decisive influences—and will sometimes be in conflict, needing ethical guidance.

- Economic forces are largely driving these developments and are themselves substantially driven by materialistic motivations, but they are also shaped by and subject to social, cultural, and spiritual influences, even if these are presently confused, inarticulate, or questionable.

- Religion invariably shapes a society's cultural and spiritual values; thus, no area of social life is purely secular, but since religion exists in the midst of social realities, it makes a great deal of difference what religion is present and how it relates to social realities.

- Economic life, as a peculiar mix of calculated interest, socio-political formation, and religio-ethical commitment, stands as a key test as to whether the future will be a blessing or a curse to humanity.

- Theological understandings of the Bible and the classic tradition, in a reconstructive dialogue with the social and human sciences, can correct religious errors, contribute to the understanding of social and economic life, and render a Christian ethic to guide the emerging world civilization.

Such issues will be pursued by the method of "apologetic dialogue." "Apologetics" is often contrasted to "dogmatics" which seeks to set forth the doctrinal teaching of the church on its own terms. Dogmatics has its important place, and will often serve as a resource to our efforts. But apologetics seeks to show when, where, and how Christian faith and ethics are intellectually and morally valid and to engage in critical and mutually corrective dialogue with those who doubt all of it from without or major parts of it from within. Since many do not know of, hold to, or care about dogmatic matters as they bear on social and economic life, we must show the significance of theology in and for public discourse.

We do this in a dialogical setting and for the dialogical settings of teaching and learning. Supported by the Project on Public Theology at Princeton Theological Seminary, funded by the Lilly Endowment and by Abingdon Press, our editorial board meets twice a year for discussion of the matters that appear in print, and each volume will have three or more perspectives on its topic. The board and all contributors are Christian, and all have studied the relationship of Christian ethics to economic life. We come from several backgrounds and traditions—Ecumenical, Evangelical, and Roman Catholic. Most are Protestant. We represent several fields of study. Some positions, however, are not represented. No one is flatly a libertarian, humanist, liberationist, or fundamentalist, although members of our group are convinced that, with proper theological qualification, each of these views could make a contribution to some aspect of our thought together. Taken alone, we believe, each of these views tends to be reductionistic, dishonest, and unfaithful. Yet, we also suspect that each of these views poses a question that must be answered: What preserves individual dignity and freedom? What place ought Christianity to give to humanist values and to the place of humanity in the plenitude of creation? What serves the poor and the oppressed and helps us understand the reasons for their situations? And, what is fundamental in faith and morals?

We are believers seeking to identify the ethics required for economic and social reconstruction, less like those who write party platforms to vent opinion or gain power than those who write briefs in and for a collegium of individuals who are attempting to adjudicate important matters from different angles of view, to plumb deeper, to seek a truer view, and to find a better way for the common life. We invite all who will to join us.

Max L. Stackhouse
General Editor

Already Published

Volume 1: *Christian Social Ethics in a Global Era*
Max L. Stackhouse, with Peter L. Berger,
Dennis P. McCann, and M. Douglas Meeks

Volume 2: *Environmental Ethics and Christian Humanism*
Thomas Sieger Derr, with James A. Nash
and Richard John Neuhaus

In Preparation

Volume 4: *Organization Man, Organization Woman:
Calling, Leadership, and Culture*
Shirley J. Roels, with Barbara Hilkert Andolsen
and Paul F. Camenisch

Other Volumes to be Announced

Introduction

Max L. Stackhouse

At the turn of the last century, as the effects of industrialization spread from England to the European continent and to North America, a great number of social analysts, social ethicists, cultural critics, philosophers, and theologians began to wrestle with the implications of the new worldwide connections that were at hand. After all, the steamship and the transatlantic cable brought neighbors across the sea closer to one another. The reports of missionaries, traders, explorers, and the emerging science of anthropology engaged many with their treatments of other people, other religions, other customs, and other ways of organizing life. And the rush to carve up the worlds that European adventurers had only recently discovered eventuated in a colonialism in which economic interests, imperial lusts for power, religious zeal, and the felt obligation to "civilize" other peoples were inextricably intertwined. Falteringly, inadequately, often pompously, people began to think each other's thoughts (or what they thought were other's thoughts) and construct general theories of world history and a cosmopolitan civilization. Surely, the myriad of forces that had generated modernity would bring the world to a new unity.

One of the distinct features of this period was the new attention that was given to economic life as a discrete area of human activity. Of course, from time immemorial, hunters and gatherers, farmers and herders, exploiters and rulers had developed organized ways of extracting enough resources from the earth, or from the less powerful, to build and sustain communities and empires. But these activities were connected to family, to household, clan, tribe, or relatively modest collections of some combination of these. Now, at geometrically increasing rates, economic institutions outside these constraints (nascently present for centuries) began to be formed—trading companies, family firms distinct from the family itself, joint stock enterprises, incorporated entities with standing as a *persona ficta* before the law, and the like. They were no longer subservient to family interests alone, or even fully governed by the state; they had an independence of organization, purpose, and polity. These new entities, generically called corporations, were seen as something of a problem, for they disrupted old modes of production and changed social relationships dramatically, but the modes of analysis of them were not clear.

A number of scholars with distinctive loyalties began to develop theories of the pluralistic "sectors" of modern, differentiated societies and to treat the economic life and the new institutions in which it was increasingly embedded in the context of what was earlier called "civil society," a term used by the ancient Stoics, adopted by some at the times of the English and French revolutions that established democracy, and returned to frequent usage in only the last few years. One thinks of the "religiously unmusical" Max Weber, as his wife said of his personal convictions, who spoke often about the rationalization and secularization of the various "departments of life" as the context (historically shaped by particular religious influences) in which to interpret the "universally significant" economic developments of the West. Closely linked to him and using similar terms was the liberal Lutheran Ernst Troeltsch, who explored economic issues as *the* "social question" in university, church, and political activities. The conservative Calvinist Abraham Kuyper, who later also became prime minister of Holland, developed a parallel theory of the relative sovereignty of the various "spheres" of human existence in Creation, and wrote powerfully about the needs of workers and the rights of management, while opposing any "revolutionary" strategies, such as the memories of the French Revolution had suggested to the advocates of secular socialism. Meanwhile, Leo XIII engendered a new tradition of "social encyclicals" in the Roman Catholic Church that spoke theologically to these issues, and called for a recognition of the distinct and inviolable roles of a number of institutions in society, family, church, labor, industry, and political regime. And the Social Gospel Movement, especially under the influence of Walter Rauschenbusch, developed a pluralist theory of society and called for the actualization of moral social relationships in the unbridled world of business.

All of these authors had suggestive but undeveloped views of corporations and their role in both economic development and civil society generally. Most were quite reserved about their importance or morality.

The peculiarly short and violent period of time between then and now, which we call the twentieth century, but which in many senses only began with World War I in 1914 and ended in 1989 with the end of the cold war, did not fulfill the dreams of world unity held by our forebears of a century ago. Nor did the focus on economic life and corporate development in the context of pluralistic civil society dominate the minds and hearts of the best theologians, ethicists, and social interpreters. Instead, questions of political power seized the center of attention, and economic life was relegated, in may ways, to the back seat, subordinate to them. The analytic and moral examination of the corporation played a secondary, and suspect, role in dominant doctrines of political economy. This was true whether one spoke of the National Socialist nihilism of Fascist Western Europe; of the Soviet Socialist command economies of Eastern Europe; of the colonialist policies of the great northern and western nations; of the one-party, quasi-socialist policies of the post-colonial southern and eastern nations of the mercantilist structures of authoritarian regimes; or of the New Deal forms of "welfare capitalism" that came to characterize much of the "century."

Now, on the brink of a new century and facing the relative decline of most of the political ideologies and military forces that terrorized the intervening century of blood and bombs and steel, we begin to note, again, the geometric increase of the power of the modern business corporation. And our ambivalence about it is that we protest its bigness and simultaneously criticize it for downsizing. Yet, no assessment of the realities of our times would be complete without careful attention to its pervasive influence—and, indeed, its simultaneous independence of the authority of national governments and increased dependence on, and reorganization of, civil society. Even more, no ethical analysis of contemporary civilization could fail to focus directly on the moral character, the promise, and the perils brought by this structural transformation of the common life, one that now is not only American or Western, but international and global.

In this volume, David Krueger, already a noted author and teacher in business ethics at a relatively young age, takes up a number of the critical issues that have to be faced regarding these newly influential institutions and the theological, moral, and societal

13

context in which they are best understood and guided to contribute most to the common good. Among the suggestive, if controversial, perspectives he sets forth, none is quite so striking as his proposal for the concept of "productive justice." From ancient times, and in the ethical literature of most of the world's religions and cultures, people are advised to be fair in "dealings": honest weights and measures, opportunities to examine goods and instruments of payment without deception, promise-keeping, debt payment, giving a good day's work for due wages, keeping other people's money in trust, and so forth. From ancient scriptures to contemporary small-claims courts, these matters of "commutative justice" make the life of business and commerce possible. Without this form of justice, social trust, and the trustworthiness that sustains it, would degenerate into a "war of all against all," as we see in locales where these break down.

Similarly, matters of "distributive justice" have received great attention—especially since the rise of the industrial corporation of the nineteenth century that generated new classes of workers, usually quite distinct from and not seldom exploited by new classes of managers, as both theorists and advocates recognized. Perhaps no economic concept has so dominated economic ethics and social criticism at the end of the last century, and at the end of this one, as the notion of relative equality. It was almost universally presumed, if not always explicitly stated, to be the regulative principle of justice, in contrast to the principle of "to each his due," that dominated aristocratic and feudal ethics—with the understanding that those with different stations in life had different duties and claims on justice. The protest against the creation of new, polarized classes or nations became central to modern morality. People do not want, and think that God does not want, a society dominated by the super-rich who do not have to be concerned about the common good, and populated by the marginalized poor who can only struggle to survive and cannot contribute to the common good. The various political programs of socialism and welfare, from the New Deal to the War on Poverty, and most forms of "liberation theology" as it was informally adopted by much church leadership, were dedicated to this distributive definition of justice.

Out of his intense involvements both with corporations in North America and with populist movements in Central America, David Krueger became convinced that the concern for the poor was right, both morally and theologically; but he also became convinced that the analysis of the role of the corporations in this situation was more often wrong than right. Corporations had more promise for the solution to the problems than was allowed in most analyses, and they were less guilty of causing the problems than was claimed. The intense criticism of the modern business corporations simply did not grasp the moral character of production, or the distinctive morality of corporate units, which is different from that of family or state.

On this basis, Krueger here sets forth a creative and bold proposal, one that can and should be taken up in many debates. He offers a theologically and empirically rooted, ethically ordered concept of "productive justice" as a contemporary addition to the classically known concepts of "commutative" and "distributive" justice. The former is necessary in all of civil society, the latter may be the special province of government; but he makes a strong case for the distinctive character of productive justice proper to the new institutions, the corporations, that dominate business and economic activity today around the world.

The critical assessment of this proposal begins immediately. Don Shriver, one of the noted senior statesmen in the field of Christian social ethics, with wide experience in both hands-on engagement and scholarly analysis of relevant issues, applauds the effort—with two cheers, not three—and poses, in a collegial, but sharp way, two challenges to the idea. While the concept of "productive justice" presumes to be theologically rooted, it is not at all clear to Shriver that the biblical warrants are fully clear. Indeed, some of the key biblical texts that come to mind may even oppose parts of what Krueger is proposing. And Shriver wonders whether the concept is, or can be, so construed as to make it supportive of what seems to be the growing division between rich and poor in this country. In other words, does it, can it, will it sanction the violation of hard-won principles of distributive justice?

Laura Nash, another noted author who has perhaps done more analysis of the values and ethical orientations of those engaged in the management of business corporations than any other contemporary author, and who comes at these issues more from the perspective of the business school than the divinity school, also offers a critical response. First of all, she challenges the rather benign reading of the emerging global situation she finds in Krueger's presentation. It seems to her much more threatening and explosive. But more than that, she wants to know how the mode of ethical analysis done by theological and social ethicists actually penetrates the operational ends of what managers do, what business does, and how things actually work. In pressing this question, she poses issues not only for Krueger, but for all those who study contemporary affairs and institutions using the tools of contemporary religious social ethics.

In a concluding rejoinder, Krueger draws a number of the lines that suggest where future debates are likely to take us. All in all, this major proposal with its discerning critics and collegial interaction points us in directions that surely cannot be avoided in the coming decades.

Chapter 1

The Business Corporation and Productive Justice in the Global Economy

David A. Krueger

Introduction

The New Social Context of Business

Business corporations, and the world around them, are changing rapidly. The collapse of the cold war, a nearly global rejection of centrally planned economies and the concurrent strengthening of market-based institutions and practices; the outward, if unsteady, expansion of pluralistic, constitutional democracy; a redefining and downsizing of the role of government in society; continued movements toward global economic integration and trade liberalization; an explosion of new technologies (product, process, communication)—all of these trends are dramatically influencing societies and business corporations around the globe. These changes beg for fresh Christian ethical thinking—both generally with respect to our Christian social identity and our visions of the good society, and more specifically with respect to the role of the Christian in economic life and our visions of the proper role of business in society.

The attempt to provide a fresh approach to business corporations in a global market economy from the standpoint of Christian ethics is complicated by the fact that, as many say, we live in a post-modern society—our systems of meaning are many and varied. This fact is nowhere more true than in how we understand and interpret Christian faith and ethics. Structures of religious meaning and authority that were once thought be to monolithic and authoritarian in some parts of the globe now seem more fragmented and dispersed as we become more familiar with other cultures and religions. We are many voices and not one, and yet more remarkable than our variety is the quest for unity among our diversity. This treatment of Christian ethics seeks to aid that effort to find a more integrated normative vision and critical assessment of the role of the business corporation in today's global economy. My argument makes choices at various levels—how I portray theology and faith, what ethical concepts I emphasize, how I describe larger macroeconomic trends in the global economy, how I view the role of the corporation in society, how I see life within the corporation, how I draw moral conclusions in light of all these methodological elements. Other arguments and conclusions are of course possible and would turn on different choices at various levels. Those who contest my claims will diverge at one or more points in my argument.

My general argument is that the Christian faith can provide a transformative ethic of responsibility that enables Christians to envision the purposes and activities of economic life generally and business corporations specifically as vital to the development of the good society. This ethic helps shape a normative vision of corporate purpose and provides substantive criteria for evaluating the performance and practices of the business corporation in a global market economy. Failure to engage the modern business corporation suggests that some spheres of human activity that will decisively shape our future are outside of God's sovereignty and care or beyond the reach of Christian moral reflection. It commits the faith to some form of sectarian withdrawal, which neglects a moral seriousness that seeks to help people who work in these institutions that will be so pivotal in shaping the common life of the next century.

Can Christianity Speak To These Changes?

Twentieth-century Christian ethics has had little constructive or positive to say about the modern business corporation until quite recently. Its analysis tended to focus at more abstract levels of economic systems and political economy. It, like political rhetoric in the cold war, was usually embroiled in debates about the relative moral merits of capitalism and socialism as general systems for organizing economic production and distribution. Indeed, most of the classic figures who shaped the ethical thinking of the century—Rauschenbusch, Tillich, Reinhold Niebuhr, Brunner, Gutiérrez—exhibited, at least for some major period of their careers, a radical suspicion of "capitalist" economic arrangements, either rejecting capitalism outright in favor of socialism, or, short of wholesale rejection, holding that it needed substantial restraint and correction, largely through government intervention. If the latter, business corporations were viewed reluctantly as necessary evils to be tolerated (short of communism, which was usually deemed worse), yet always to be held in great suspicion and mistrust, because of the social power and usually dangerous values that they embodied and transmitted to society. Often, corporations were assumed to be the mother, or the child (which was not quite clear), of greed, acquisitiveness, materialism, narrow "economic rationality," and individualism. They also generated harmful social effects: maldistributions of wealth and income, with massive acquisitions of wealth side by side with pockets of squalid poverty; disruption of traditional social patterns of community; the perpetuation of racism and sexism; pollution; and international neocolonialism. In spite of these general aspersions, one finds within the literature virtually no concrete discussion of business corporations. Actual corporations are rarely, if ever, mentioned by name. Their activities are rarely described and analyzed in detail. Instead, the primary unit of analysis is more general and abstract, focusing on capitalism as a system.

This negative appraisal of business corporations was coupled with deep suspicions about other basic dimensions of economic life attributed to capitalism—the acquisition and accumulation of wealth (in the forms of both capital and consumption), the activity of trading within markets, and the institution of profits. Our focus was usually transfixed on political economy and viewed through a particular set of lenses that raised only certain questions, such as "How can the countervailing forces of government and other third sector institutions be assembled to restrain the socially dangerous tendencies of markets, wealth accumulation, business corporations, and the acquisition of corporate profits?" Both positions—the wholesale rejection of the capitalist system and the suspicious toleration of a substantially restrained capitalism—had much the same outcome with respect to ethical judgments and constructive prescriptions about business corporations themselves: virtual silence, little attention to detailed analysis of corporate activity, and often intense hostility.

This is not to argue that some aspects of these criticisms were unjustified—there has been much to criticize in the emergence and evolution of capitalism in the past century. Indeed, there are inherent tensions between aspects of our Christian tradition and modern economic developments. Scripture honors those who use wealth wisely and compassionately, but also warns against the temptations of wealth and laments social practices that oppress the poor and powerless in society. But sometimes drawing uncritically on these positive or negative evaluations, parts of the tradition may have been misguided, often due to inadequate or even confused analyses about the appropriate uses and distributions of power in society. In our day, we must ask to what extent did these mainstream and liberationist thinkers within our tradition seek inappropriately or inordinately to apply a political commitment to democratic decision making to economic life? Did they sometimes naively assume that the modern moral commitment to democratic decision making could be uniformly applied to politics and economics? Or that the political realm could easily democratize economic decision making in pursuit of the common good in ways that markets could not? In sum, much of this negative moral assessment of twentieth-century capitalist business corporations seems to have been the result of a confusion about the appropriate uses and differentiation of power between a democratic political order and a market economic order, both of which seem essential for the development of a healthy civil society, as well as due to lopsided readings of biblical texts.

In sum, in our century, precious little attention was devoted to the development of a substantive Christian ethic for capitalism and the modern business corporation.[1] With the collapse of the previous capitalist-socialist bipolar world and the emergence of a new economic context, Christianity is thus faced with the hard question of asking itself whether it has anything substantive to say about the normative purposes and ordering of business corporations in a global market economy.

The moral problem of the twenty-first century will likely not be oppressive, monistic structures of meaning and authority; this was the twentieth century's problem—fascism, totalitarianism, statism, etc., which subjugated freedom to inappropriate and excessive structures of meaning and authority. Rather, our problem may be the *absence* of meaning and authority—inordinate freedom unrestrained by any compelling or coherent systems of belief and authority. With respect to economic life, the threat to market-based systems and corporations will less likely be *false* religion (e.g., placing hopes for social transformation in Marxism and centralized planning) than it will be *no* religion—that is, economic activity that is inadequately shaped by larger religious/metaphysical/normative visions of what constitutes a good earth, society, and person.

Indeed, not only has Marxism and centralized planning collapsed as a "religious" worldview vying for our deepest human affirmation and consent, but the rhetoric of capitalism as a system of meaning and "salvation" as well seems to have waned as an ideological construct outwardly vying for our allegiance in the arena of public debate. With the cold war over, the war of words and meaning has also dissipated. We no longer attack or defend capitalism as we did in the previous era, but are more likely merely to assume it as a fundamental part of our social reality, like constitutional democracy and electronic entertainment, if not quite like sex and death. Now that the "false god" of socialism has crumbled, we are also less likely to define capitalism with such grandiose and dangerously idolatrous religious language as well. Hence, my aim is not a moral defense of the ideology of "capitalism" and the business corporations that serve as its "engines," if by capitalism we mean a deified economic order that is beyond moral fault or that is presumed good without careful appeal to the evidence of history. Nor do I mean some social structure that glorifies unrestrained freedom and individual liberty, wealth, and the accumulation of profits at the expense of all other social values and pursuits. Nor do I mean a social structure that elevates economic rationality above all others, choking out other dimensions of human fulfillment and social organization. These are all false ideologies, unsustainable by a Christian vision of life.

Rather, I mean more modestly to argue that we may now be at an historical moment when we are better able to put economic life and institutions in their proper religious and moral perspective—as penultimately and not ultimately important sources of meaning and value for our lives and society; as potential signs of grace and as institutional arenas within which to live out our callings as Christians in the world, but not as gods of ultimate salvation. This permits us to construct more integrated, yet differentiated, theological understandings of human and social purpose that place economic institutions and activities in their proper place.

However, it is not clear that the contemporary church can construct and nurture such a sustainable vision of civil society among many competing worldviews and notions of the good society that will be sufficiently compelling to enough people to "make a difference." It is not obvious that contemporary Christian theology is yet up to the task, for this will require a "sea change" in its general orientation and tone. Constructing an ethic for modern corporate life, then, demands also an inquiry into and a reconstruction of theology. What resources might it provide and how might it attempt to embody that vision within the fabric of economic institutions and practices in a global economy?

The question for Christian social ethics no longer is what type of economic system we should choose. While it is true that history may yet bring what we cannot now imagine, and that it once seemed as recently as 1929 that capitalism was finished, it now seems beyond dispute that fundamental market-based institutions are more or less being put into place around the globe. The seductions of socialism (national, proletarian, communist) have passed. Nor is the question whether we can decisively restrain, or even stop the inexorable macro trends shaping the global economy. Global integration and technological innovations and revolutions will continue to transform economic life whether we attempt artificial, stop-gap political constraints or not.

This is not to suggest a mechanistic world in which humans are "out of control." But it is to argue that there are limits to how humans manage that process. As technology becomes dispersed and economic integration more widespread, single actors, be they nation state governments or individual corporations, will have less capacity unilaterally to shape those trends. Rather, effective efforts to manage the outcomes of this process will need to be more collaborative and multisectoral than in the past, for example through multilateral and regional treaties and trade agreements. While setbacks will undoubtedly occur (e.g., occasional protectionist pressures), they will face ever stronger countervailing trends that will make such efforts self-defeating.

Rather, the question is not what economic system to choose but what larger moral purposes, vision, and values global society will employ to construct, direct, and evaluate the institutions and practices of a global market economy. This includes the activities and conduct of business corporations, as well as the roles of governments and other social institutions that seek to shape and restrain corporate scopes of action.

For Christians, this moral question becomes both theological and strategic. Theologically, it asks whether we can articulate a larger theologically grounded normative vision of the proper purpose of the business corporation within the good society and an ecologically sustainable world. If we can, it also becomes strategic, for we must then ask whether and how this theological vision might become practical (i.e., public theology). How can we employ our deepest religious values about the nature of social reality in ways that actually shape the fabric of civilization, in particular the structures and institutions of economic life? How can the beliefs and values of Christian faith shape and transform the intentions and actions of Christians who shape, direct, manage, survive (and fail) within those structures and organizations? I mean this as no rhetorical question, for Christianity's strongest danger in the twenty-first century may be a growing irrelevance in matters social and economic. While the basic institutional fabric and framework of Western society and its enduring economic institutions may have been strongly shaped by religious values at a time when religion played a more pronounced role for individuals and society, those presumed religious roots now may be replaced by others. While economic freedom (at least for some individuals) arguably was restrained and shaped by a larger vision of vocation—holiness and order—now we face the threat of freedom unrestrained by moral vision.

The Modern Business Corporation

For many decades, the limited liability business corporation has been the dominant institution for conducting economic activity within most industrialized Western countries. With the continued dismantling of centrally planned economies of the former Second World, as well as public sector economies of the Third World, the business corporation's global reach and social impact will only grow. In addition, various social, economic, and technological factors are dramatically changing the character and structure of life within it. Demilitarization, technological change (in products, processes, and communications), global trade liberalization and integration, increased global competition, increased multiculturalism and diversity within the workplace, the democratizing of political life globally, and government downsizing, which is changing the nature of business/government relationships and regulation—all these internal and external factors combine to make life within the business corporation perhaps more highly dynamic than ever before. How we understand the purpose of the business corporation, the scope of these changes, the corporation's social and environmental impacts on the world around it, its future prospects and trends—all of these are highly contestable topics subject to radically different descriptive and analytic accounts and interpretations.

It is well beyond the scope of this essay to provide a comprehensive and detailed portrayal of the modern business corporation, its various internal components, and its various impacts on the larger society. At best we can acknowledge its centrality for modern post-socialist, global market society as well as the growing complexity of factors that influence its roles and activities. It is clear that Christians and others in society will continue to hold differing and sometimes radically conflicting views about modern business corporations and how to best describe and analyze them. Nevertheless, at least one imperative is clear for Christians and the Christian community—we must devote more, not less, careful and detailed attention to this increasingly vital institution in global society. It may not be a resident of the "New Jerusalem" but it is here "for the long-term." Whatever abstracted portrayals we use to characterize the corporation, it is where most people—our friends, neighbors, fellow Christians—spend much of their waking lives. The concrete reality is that it is within the corporation that lives are shaped, challenged, fail, and succeed. It is here where people's careers are developed or thwarted, and where many of our views of the fairness or unfairness of the world are formed. It is one of the places where we are nurtured and supported, or feel threatened and rejected, respected or harassed. It is where people form friendships and animosities, and fall in love at the water cooler and the lunch table. Thus, if Christianity is to be a vital, transformative force in this world, it behooves us to diagnose, dissect, and analyze the corporation more deeply and carefully than our tradition has in the past.

The Quest for Basic Normative Standards

As a global society, we are in an historic period of transition as we re-examine and redefine the roles and responsibilities of society's primary institutions—multilateral organizations such as the United Nations, the World Bank, the International Monetary Fund, and the

World Trade Organization; governments and the nation-state itself; economic institutions; even religious institutions and the family. To a large extent, this rethinking and restructuring is driven by the trend toward global integration, which will affect the governance roles and responsibilities of both political and economic institutions. Global integration of economic activity means that unilateral power shifts toward multilateral power and authority, for governments and business corporations alike. In both spheres, this trend implies the growing role and importance of standards of behavior that stand beyond single social actors. In the political realm, nation-states will be increasingly held accountable to multilateral norms, standards, and regulations, for instance through regional and international treaties and protocols. This makes world organizations such as the World Bank and the United Nations more, rather than less, important, even as regional forms of collaboration such as the North American Free Trade Association (NAFTA) and the European Union also expand. It also means that corporations will be held accountable to standards of behavior that are also increasingly multilateral and collaborative, making organizations such as the World Trade Organization even more important.

This fundamental probing includes a fresh asking of the question, What normative expectations can and should we rightly place on the business corporation in a global market society? This is a basic question that Christians must consider if we are to have an effective transformative influence upon the future shape of civil society in the twenty-first century. Yet this task—the formulation of a Christian ethic for business—itself begs four questions about the purposes of economic life with which we must wrestle: (1) To what extent is it permissible, indeed even mandated, to create wealth (creating goods and services as well as accumulating wealth for savings and investment)? (2) To what extent is it permissible, even commendable, to participate in market activities, notably the buying and selling of goods and services? (3) To what extent is it permissible, even commendable, to work within business corporations? and (4) To what extent is it permissible, even commendable, to generate profits?

These four economic activities—creating wealth, trading in markets, working within corporations, and making profits—lie at the heart of economic life today. They are fundamental and indeed unavoidable within the contours of today's global market economy. Yet they all have a "checkered past" in terms of theological evaluation within our Christian tradition. This essay, therefore, will attempt to offer both positive theological and ethical grounds for participation in these four economic activities as well as discussion of their appropriate moral limits. On the one hand, we must provide the positive grounds for arguing that these activities offer the primary institutional opportunities and conditions for Christians and others to exercise responsibility within economic life. On the other hand, we must articulate the essential limits to these activities, the violation or overstepping of which can lead to irresponsibility, violations of human dignity, and social and ecological disorder.

(1) *Wealth Creation.* If we have learned anything from the collapse of socialism, it is that some global consensus exists about what we desire from economic institutions—that the material aspirations of people be advanced in a broad-based way that permits high levels of economic freedom and individual initiative (and also in ways that create less rather than more environmental destruction). In other words, with proper moral conditions as well as constraints, we must affirm as morally good the basic aspirations of people around the world for material well-being. This quest necessarily requires the creation and accumulation of wealth within society. The satisfaction of material needs is not supremely or ultimately important for persons or societies. As Christians we can affirm that right relationship with God (salvation) and the character and quality of our lives together—our common life—are pursuits of higher importance than our relationships with and accumulation of material things. But material goods are nevertheless vitally important. While we "do not live by bread alone," it is also true that life is not possible without bread.

The satisfaction of material needs is *the* fundamental role of economic systems generally, and of business corporations specifically, within our current market-based global economy. In a global society in which a large percentage of people still remain poor, some desperately poor, it follows logically that a higher level of global economic output and wealth is a morally defensible goal. Even if we argue for structural mechanisms that aim at redistribution from rich to poor, the creation of wealth is still presupposed. In some sense, we must not assert the moral slogan proposed by some that "less is better," but rather that "more is better" and "less is worse." Furthermore, we must reject the role of religion in society if that religion serves to generate more, rather than less, poverty.

I am not arguing that all current economic structures, institutions, rules, and practices are just, nor that all types of wealth accumulation and economic consumption are conducive to the moral life or the good society, nor that there is not gratuitous waste in the production and allocation of wealth (both socially and ecologically). But I am arguing, at least on a minimal level, that business corporations, undergirded by the system of institutional rules and cultural norms and conditions that support them, must face the social, and indeed moral, challenge to be even more effective in producing goods and services in a broad-based way around the globe. By "broad-based," I mean the capacity to meet at least the basic material needs of the majority of people, especially within the less developed world, in ways that respect human dignity, demonstrate justice, and seek ecological sustainability. Advancing this morally laden social purpose requires that we turn our attention to productive justice, and a consideration of the ethical conditions for expanding economic output globally in ways that contribute to the alleviation of poverty and the creation of just and ecologically sustainable human communities.

In a sense, this argument in support of enhanced wealth creation globally flies in the face of a fundamental assumption that shaped the construction of much of social life in the twentieth century. That premise, espoused by both Marxism and to some extent by the Western liberalism that spawned the welfare state, was that the institutional and technological advances of industrial capitalism had produced enough economic output to meet the basic material needs of all people. Since we had "solved" the problem of production, we could devote our attention primarily to distribution. Hence, in both systems, the state became the primary mechanism for the redistribution of a sufficiently large economic pie. The ethic for which I am arguing here stands against this assumption, asserting instead that our global "economic pie" must expand, rather than remain constant or even contract, if we are to create a sustainable global society. Hence, the creation and expansion of wealth, in the form of capital accumulation, becomes an essential, but not sufficient, institutional ingredient for that moral task.

(2) *Competitive Markets.* Recent economic trends also suggest a strong global consensus about the positive role of markets in generating material and social well-being. We must avoid the temptation to idolize markets, assuming them to be some easy savior that magically creates wealth and prosperity or that necessarily creates morally desirable distributions of wealth and income. But we should also avoid the opposite error of omission—of ignoring their seemingly universal capacity to serve as a more effective primary institutional means to allocate goods and services than twentieth century's other grand allocative experiment—centralized planning.

Markets are ubiquitous. People trade in nearly all social contexts, from highly regulated and formalized settings such as the pits of commodities exchanges to informal settings such as prisons and children's playgrounds. Across the globe, people want to trade, and to do so within boundaries that define moral fairness. Around the world, nation-states that had moved away from markets during the twentieth century are now taking systemic steps to institutionalize them through protective legal frameworks, the downsizing of public sector economic activity, and efforts that aim to stimulate the development of competitive private sectors that function in increasingly unprotected free markets. Hence, Christian ethics must come to terms with the need for a conditional defense of market mechanisms and safeguards which attempt to create and protect the relatively free movement of prices for goods and services within competitive markets.

(3) *Working in Corporations.* Within industrialized countries, most workers are employed in the private sector by business corporations. How should we interpret the role and impacts of corporations on society and the natural world?[2] Are corporations primarily a source of exploitative power, tending to generate harmful impacts on various groups and on society as a whole? If so, there would be little reason to advocate that Christians should participate in them. Nor would there be much in terms of constructive advice about how best to conduct oneself in such a role. On the contrary, if Christianity is to develop an ethic of transformative engagement with the global market economy, it must seek a more constructive and nuanced view of the role of business corporations in the world today. We must seek to articulate a constructive vision for corporate purpose and articulate the positive conditions under which Christians ought rightly to participate within business corporations, while at the same time not be blind to the actual and potential threats that corporations can pose to the interests of others and the common good.

(4) *Making Profits.* Profits are the rationally calculated increase of assets that remains in a corporation after all business expenses have been paid. These assets may be converted to cash or other instruments of exchange and may be distributed to owners or retained by the corporation for future investment. How should we morally assess this fundamental dimension of market economies? Do we consider profits to be the result of greed, which corrupts the human heart? Do profits represent the accumulation of private interests and power at the expense of public interests? Or do we consider profits as a legitimate measure of a corporation's performance and contribution to society? Again, if Christianity is to shape an ethic for the global market economy, it must come to terms with the institution of profit and clarify its appropriate moral conditions and limits.

This essay suggests how Christian ethics can enter into that debate about the proper role of business in society. What substantive contributions can Christian ethics make in the shaping of a normative ethic for business corporations in a global economy? A Christian ethic for the global economy of the twenty-first century must come to terms with the creation of wealth, trading in markets, work in corporations, and the generation of profits. How can these activities become opportunities for Christian vocation in the world? Under what positive conditions should we support these activities? And what are the appropriate negative limits and constraints on these activities? Because the Christian faith affirms a larger vision of the social good, business performance also should be judged not merely by the criterion of profitability but also to some extent by its capacity to realize that larger good in ways that make qualitative and not only quantitative contributions. Thus, the basic purpose of economic life generally, and of business corporations specifically, is to generate wealth for society in ways that are consistent with a theologically informed vision of the common good. This pursuit of wealth, in the form of goods and services, is properly guided and restrained by at least the following five moral considerations: (1) that it be efficient (and thus profitable and competitive); (2) that its products be beneficial and not harmful to users and society; (3) that in its relations with various constituent or stakeholder groups, it adhere to basic standards of productive justice; (4) that it support the creation and effective administration of appropriate countervailing institutions, e.g., democratic governments, regulatory agencies, and non-governmental organizations (NGOs), whose combined efforts aim to realize the well-functioning of civil society; and (5) that its activities aim toward environmental sustainability and sustainable development. Together, these moral criteria function to define the conditions of productive justice in a global market economy. We must now turn our attention both to the theological formulation for such a vision, and to a more detailed explanation of its ethical components.

Theological Bases for an Ethic of "Productive Justice"

A Christian ethic for the modern business corporation must be theologically rooted. This ethic should be consistent with a larger normative vision of global civil society, from which we can specify the proper purposes of the business corporation for the simple reason that Christians believe that God's reign extends over the whole world, even when it is in rebellion against God's laws and purposes. This requires that we use Christian theology to make substantive claims about the good society, the proper roles of social institutions including business, and the appropriate roles and responsibilities of persons within business.

One of the most helpful ways of speaking about these matters today is the call for an "ethic of responsibility," especially as set forth in our times by H. Richard Niebuhr. It has several main parts: A key ingredient depends on a theology of conversion that acknowledges both human capacities for good (transformation grounded in grace) and for evil (inordinate egoism based upon sin), especially as these are connected to the notion of the common good. In *Christ and Culture*, Niebuhr outlined various ways that prominent Christian thinkers and theological traditions have understood the connections between Christian belief and social practice. This classic typology of Christian social ethics can also serve as a conceptual "road map" of diverse ways that one might relate Christian ethics to contemporary capitalist business practice. These five positions can be described as (1) "prophetic/perfectionist," which understands the ethical imperatives of Christian faith as predominantly inconsistent with capitalism (e.g., most forms of liberation theology); (2) "accommodative," which would assert either that Christian ethical norms are *de facto* embodied within capitalism or that such norms have no relevance to economic and business life, e.g., some tendencies within fundamentalist and pietist Protestant positions; (3) "incarnational/synthetist," which affirms the achievements of a rightly ordered capitalism but which sees its perfection as well as ultimate human fulfillment standing beyond it and accessible only through faith and revelation (e.g., modern papal social thought on economic life); (4) "dualist/paradoxical," which asserts both the ever-present corruptibility and corruption of capitalism, falling dismally short of the divine intentions, as well as its ever-present possibility as a social reality appropriate for the preservation of human life that may become a more or less justly ordered community within which service to the neighbor is lived out (e.g., classical Lutheran "two kingdoms" social ethics, and many contemporary Evangelicals); and (5) "transformative/conversionist," which understands capitalism and business practice to be flawed and marred by sin but open to the possibility of renewal and creative transformation under the sovereignty of God.[3]

While all five of these positions have shown their faces prominently within recent discussions about economic life, I believe that the last three will likely become the prevailing Christian ethical positions in the coming era. The "dualist/paradoxical" position is widely held among minority Christians, for example, and the "incarnational/synthetist" position is reflected in much Roman Catholic thought, such as John Paul II's 1991 encyclical *Centesimus Annus*, with its tendency to engage in the construction of substantive ethical edifices, backed by epistemological, methodological, and anthropological assumptions that assert the human capacity to know and do such things. The "transformative/conversionist" approach, which I will develop, is more in accord with classical Augustinian and Reformation traditions, with their tendency to engage in a more critical assessment, backed by their own assumptions about God, the limits of human knowledge, and the role of sin in the world. While I am advocating the transformative position as most potentially fruitful for modern economic life, especially within the Protestant tradition, I also acknowledge the potential uses of other positions. We must also, therefore, consider how Christian ethics makes strategic choices among Niebuhr's types to guide action within economic life and within business corporations, a matter that I briefly and illustratively address at the end of this section.

Represented in Niebuhr's "Christ the transformer of culture" type, this conversionist approach emphasizes the fallen character of creation, and thus the partial, fragmentary, and fragile nature of human truth and human achievements, to the extent that all cultural achievements are vulnerable to error, perversion, and evil. "No synthesis—since it consists of fragmentary, historical, and hence of relative formulations of the law of creation, with acknowledgedly fragmentary previsions of the law of redemption—can be otherwise than provisional and symbolic" and thus subject "to the radical evil present in all human work" (1975, pp. 145, 148). While conversionists assert that sin "is deeply rooted in the human soul," and thus pervades all cultural achievements, they also believe "that such culture is under God's sovereign rule, and that the Christian must carry on cultural work in obedience to the Lord" (p. 191). Hence, humans are to respond to and embody within their own work the creative, ordering work of God. While culture is corrupted, it is, as Augustine argued centuries ago and many believe the Bible teaches, corrupted order; it is perverted good, not evil. "The problem of culture is therefore the problem of its conversion, not of its replacement by a new creation; though the conversion is so radical that it amounts to a kind of rebirth" (p. 194). With God, all things are affirmed to be possible in a history that is a dramatic interaction between God and humanity. Culture is always susceptible to transformation by the regeneration of the human spirit in and to the glory of God and because it exists within the world of grace, God's kingdom (pp. 196, 256).

With respect to capitalism, the transformative position interprets its achievements as the embodiment of both sin and goodness. Its goodness is perverted, its order corrupted. The Christian's moral imperative is not to work for its replacement by another fundamentally different system of production and distribution, such as a centrally planned economy, but for its conversion. Hence, unlike liberation theology, the transformationist does not advocate radical structural change of the means of production within the current historical period. Because capitalism exists under the sovereignty of God, the Christian is called to participate within it, working for its regeneration and transformation, but with the epistemological humility that is necessary given the partial and fragmentary nature of human knowing and acting. Hence, this affirmation of both divine sovereignty and moral ambiguity (the Christian realist's acknowledgment of the permanent co-existence of both goodness and sin) results in a "tipping of the scales" toward the system's fundamental goodness rather than its fundamental sinfulness or corruption. Its goodness is perverted, its order corrupted, but still goodness and order nonetheless. This implies a strategy of constructive engagement and hopeful transformation rather than wholesale rejection. (In this sense, the transformative position might tend toward greater optimism than some readings of the more Lutheran "paradoxical" position in creating and sustaining economic structures and practices that embody the divine intentions for human life in society.)

This position generally coheres with the Protestant social ethics of classic figures such as Luther and Calvin who argued for the existence of "orders of creation" or "departments of life" within which societies and their members must order and organize their social roles and moral responsibilities. In other words, we discern that there are some fundamental, divinely sanctioned institutions through which societies rightly organize their life together (e.g., family, work and economy, government, religion) and that provide the moral context and framework—the "givenness"—within which we seek to live out the moral life in all its various social dimensions, and without which human flourishing and social justice would not be possible. (This position overlaps considerably, then, with the Roman Catholic tradition's legacy of a natural order at least partially available to human knowledge and practice.) This is not to deny that there are times when regimes and institutions can become so corrupted that we can and must denounce them as severely unjust, if not evil (e.g., Nazi Germany, tyrannical aspects of Stalinist Communism, the apartheid regime in South Africa). Such situations and contexts may require strategies other than the transformative one. But even these radically corrupt examples are judged as perversions of a social norm that has some basic characteristics that are widely shared by most persons and societies as necessary for social order. For instance, the institution of family carries some norms and prohibitions which seem universal, or nearly so, even in the midst of wide cultural diversity—polygamy is almost universally prohibited; the innocent lives of children are (or should be) protected from violence and abuse; incest is proscribed. Within economic life, some norms of fairness and trust in transactions are essential. Hence, stealing and fraud are prohibited almost without exception around the globe.

Within the current historical period, economic life is constituted and shaped predominantly by market-oriented institutional arrangements and practices. I argue that the "givenness" of these arrangements, at least for the foreseeable future, implies some moral "weight" and affirmation. This moral affirmation of at least some central components of the capitalist system, albeit a critical and provisional one, further implies a moral impulse to participate within and to transform private sector institutions—most notably, limited liability business corporations—that serve as the principle mechanisms by which the capitalist system operates. Thus, the transformative position must turn its attention to the life and practice of business corporations themselves, striving to provide substantive moral content and directives for its participants, including Christians.

The transformationist's systemic moral affirmation of global market capitalism draws warrants and justification from recent historical trends and affirms them as "signs of the times." Notably, the socialist world has collapsed from within. This occurrence cannot be interpreted by Christians and others in a morally neutral or irrelevant way. It is not merely that capitalism's primary competing system of political economy has fallen away, leaving us with no alternatives to what some might consider an equally unethical system. Rather, it provides moral evidence to strengthen the transformationist's affirmation of the moral viability and promise of the global market economy. In his 1991 encyclical, *Centesimus Annus*, John Paul II unambiguously derides the past evils of the Soviet-imposed system in Eastern Europe as an oppression that created economic inefficiency, violated the human rights of workers, created a spiritual void, and destroyed and denigrated the most "basic virtues of economic life, such as truthfulness, trustworthiness and hard work." He goes on to claim that the events of 1989 provided "opportunities for human freedom to cooperate with the merciful plan of God who acts within history" (1991, #23–27).

The second theological resource I emphasize in this transformationist foundation is the concept of the "common good." While classically developed and used primarily within Roman Catholic theology and ethics (and thus more commonly lodged within Niebuhr's "incarnational/synthetist" type), this concept is not foreign to the development of Protestant ethics (it is found in Luther's and Calvin's uses of "two kingdoms" theology) and can be reappropriated for the construction of a corporate ethic in a global market economy. Indeed, I argue that this concept embodies much of the tradition's attempt to capture the fundamental social dimensions of the good life. Human fulfillment and social well-being are inherently related. This task of creating good community is a fundamental goal of the transformationist ethic.

Developed most fully within the Thomistic tradition of natural law, this concept is based upon the premise of human reason's capacity to know the good. This good can be discerned from reason and human experience accessible to all persons and is consistent with knowledge of the good revealed to Christians from special revelation (scripture and faith). While reason and all human knowledge are colored and corrupted by sin, these capacities are not so thoroughly corrupted that we cannot to some degree trust the knowledge that they provide about how to order human life and society. Practical reason, while flawed, is not destroyed. Furthermore, reason discerns that there are human goods shared in common that constitute the good human life, rightly ordered. Indeed, these common goods are intrinsically good, and are more important than private, instrumental goods, which are good insofar as they enable other higher aims. The common good is both personal and social. It enables the flourishing of individuals and entails human rights that protect the interests and aims of individuals. But it also asserts the inherently social nature of human beings—we fulfill ourselves fully only in relation to others. Fundamentally, we are social beings whose fulfillment requires vibrant and rich associations with others—political, economic, familial, cultural, and especially religious.

Any attempts to speak of the common good today must be highly dynamic and provisional, given the fundamental character of contemporary thought and practice. Classical theological articulations of common good language (e.g., within Thomistic natural law and Luther's two kingdoms' theology) were set within social contexts pre-dating modern democratic, capitalist institutions and modern scientific discovery. They presumed less dynamic social orders wherein social roles and expectations were fairly fixed and unchanging. To put this another way, theological contributions to the concept of the common good must also recognize the historicity and social character of all knowledge, as H. R. Niebuhr argued in another striking book (*The Meaning of Revelation*, 1960) and by our acknowledgment of the inevitable taints of self-interest in the ways we envision the common good, as his brother persuasively argued in one of the intellectual monuments of our century. (cf. Reinhold Niebuhr's *The Nature and Destiny of Man*, 1964).

These social, anthropological, and epistemological caveats need not force us into a relativist or empiricist camp that rejects the wholesale pursuit of truth and common interests. We must presume that, even in the midst of the diversity, pluralism, historicity, and change of modern social life, we can identify some continuities and commonalties of interests and values. Human interests are not so disparate that we have merely a wide collection of contending private interests beyond moral adjudication. Thus, we cannot finally be libertarians who believe that freedom is the only objective social value and that no other human pursuits or interests can be "common."

The idea of the common good, therefore, asserts that whatever the diversity and uniqueness that also constitutes the human, there is also a unity and coherence of values that shapes our essential identity. Shared values and human association are fundamental aspects of human nature. The "Law of Love" is ultimately more real than the "War of All against All." Human fulfillment and social well-being are achieved to the extent that we create and sustain social institutions and practices under the Law of Love and point toward the common good, and these institutions and practices are what today is called "civil society." Common good language also presumes that practical reason is a quality accessible to all persons across the multifaceted global terrain of religious and cultural particularity and diversity beyond the nation state, class and ethnic divisions, and distinctive historical experiences.

The concept of the common good has important implications for the ordering of economic life and for the value and meanings we rightly impute to it. First, the economy, its organizations, and our work within it become relativized insofar as the goods that it produces are instrumental and not intrinsic. Material wealth, goods and services, profits and a "healthy bottom line," while good, are only instrumentally good. They are not sufficient in themselves to create the good life or the good society. They are important, but not ultimately important. Rightly ordered, they provide the means of exchange, the material goods, and the services without which society cannot flourish. They satisfy vital material needs that enable the pursuit of more important, intrinsic human goods and purposes of civil society— political, cultural, educational, religious, etc. Indeed, as we scan the world horizon today, we note that societies without well-functioning (usually market-based) economies typically suffer not only material deprivation and lack of economic development but also a want of other social institutions that enable the good life of its citizens.

It is no coincidence that the primary concern of less developed countries is *economic* development, and that even in industrialized democracies, elections tend to be won or lost based upon economic indicators rather than other measures of social well-being, for without material resources it is very difficult to build and sustain a civil society. Hence, well-functioning corporations are vital to the good society. This fact is inescapable, both within the industrialized world, as well as within newly developing nations. Yet, insofar as their purpose is to produce economic goods, which are themselves instrumental, corporations cannot be elevated to supreme importance within society. Insofar as their purpose is to generate material well-being, they can never be affirmed as the most important institution in society, even if they are indispensable. Such deification is idolatrous and can become but a contemporary institutionalized expression of avarice, which makes the quest for "more" its own end. To the extent that corporations and the economy (like states and politics, or family and sexuality) are elevated to supreme status, they become wrongly and falsely idolized and deified. Hence, the concept of the common good requires that we affirm moral goods and purposes "higher" than the instrumental, material goods and services produced by business corporations. This relativization of money and material goods is consistent with both the biblical affirmation of the goodness of the material world and of our mandate to manage its resources for human well-being. It also acknowledges biblical warnings against money and wealth unduly exhaulted and wrongly managed. Wealth can serve as a curse and impediment not only to justice and community (right relationships with humanity and creation) but also to our own salvation (right relationship to God).

But let us not too quickly and falsely assume that the morally superior pursuit of intrinsic "common goods" forces us to renounce economic pursuits or to seek "moral" goods only in other types of social institutions. Indeed, it is wrong to assume that intrinsic goods—goods that are inherently good and that are constitutive of human fulfillment itself—cannot to some extent also be realized within business corporations. Corporations are not *merely* organizational vehicles for the creation of things; they also necessitate personal growth, human associations, relationships, and cooperation. In the process of creating instrumental goods, corporations also function as moral communities which can engender and enable the pursuit of intrinsic values and goods important to the development of persons and communities. These can include the development of professional skills and competencies, personal virtues, creativity, social skills such as teamwork and collaboration, and important social and moral values such as honesty and trustworthiness.

Hence, while the rightly ordered economy contains business corporations which permit and foster the development of intrinsic goods, we must also acknowledge the principled and structural limits to that attainment based upon the very nature of for-profit business organizations in a competitive market economy. If we affirm that the primary purpose of economic life and business organizations is to create wealth, we must acknowledge that this purpose, unlike that of other organizations, is fundamentally directed toward the creation of instrumental goods. And within a competitive market economy, that purpose is pursued with the social constraint of profitability. Hence, the extent to which business corporations can encourage and nurture intrinsic goods important to the common good of society is limited both by their basic purpose and by the constraint of profitability. This caveat is important, for it would be inappropriate to have moral expectations of business corporations for which they are not structured or which they are incapable of fulfilling. Corporations cannot be all things to all people, nor can we expect them to solve all social problems. In other words, the demand that a corporation produce goods and services at a profit will condition and limit its ability to satisfy some other moral expectations of a more intrinsic nature in the new competitive global market economy.

By way of illustration, let us consider the changing relationship between corporations and their workers. In the post-World War II steady-growth economy, U.S. business corporations provided relatively stable and long-term employment for their workers. And strong labor unions, backed by legal requirements for union-management negotiations, served as advocates for the worker's security and economic well-being. In the absence of strong global competition, a psychological pact as well as legal contracts existed between management and labor in many corporations wherein workers came to expect long-term employment with slow and steady growth in compensation in exchange for reasonably high levels of productivity. Some would argue that this psychological pact was an intrinsic good, almost a "covenant," apart from the many instrumental goods it provided: monetary compensation for workers, profits for companies, goods and services for customers. It also tended to foster a relationship of trust and stability, which can permit the nurture and development of persons over time. It created the larger institutional context for the formation of "moral community" within work organizations. (Of course there are competing interpretations of this labor/management relationship which cast labor or management, or both, in a darker moral light.)

In today's global market economy, though, this psychological pact and the contractual agreements are changing rapidly as many large corporations have reduced their workforce in response to such factors as technological change and global competition. The "pact" has been severely challenged, if not broken. What some would argue to be an intrinsic good—the long-term relationship of trust between worker and employer—has come under severe pressure. It can no longer be practiced and embodied as it was in the post-World War II era of the 1950s to the 1970s. Yet it is waning not because of some overarching "moral conspiracy" against workers or against "the common good" but for the sake of those pursuits for which those organizations were initially formed—to produce goods and services at a profit. Indeed, sometimes new pacts are formed with international workers abroad, and a broader notion of "common" is introduced into the sense of "good." Morally speaking, radically changing market conditions make the pursuit of some intrinsic goods more tenuous. In a time of declining costs and rising prices due to technological change and heightened global competition, corporate survival usually requires that the organization take steps to cut its production costs, including labor (and/or improve levels of productivity to justify the higher wage rates relative to other lower cost producers).

Also embedded within the notion of the common good are egalitarian and communitarian impulses. These impulses are based upon fundamental affirmations of equal human dignity and the inherent social nature and destiny of human life. For some Christian thinkers, these egalitarian and communitarian impulses resulted in an intuited rejection of market economies in favor of socialist arrangements which could ostensibly create systems of economic production and distribution that could more directly embody communitarian values and achieve more egalitarian results in the distribution of social wealth and income. One recalls that Walter Rauschenbusch's theology of the social gospel, centered on the social ideals of Christianity (cf. 1912, 1917), as well as Paul Tillich's religious socialism (1977), centered on the ontological and ethical elements of prophetic Christianity, both argued that the affirmation of democratic socialism was required. Yet in the aftermath of the collapse of socialist planned economies, we must ask whether the egalitarian and communitarian values they advocated can generate the resources to sustain a viable civil society over time.

One notes here the work of Michael Novak, who has argued that pluralistic societies that embrace democracy in the political sphere and markets in the economic sphere can provide the institutional conditions for the flourishing of "communitarian individualism," wherein the person becomes freely involved within a rich associational life directed toward individual and communal well-being (1984). From a Christian theological perspective, if we are to affirm the enduring legacy and applicability of the common good for a market-based society in a global economy, then we must be able to define and support the respects in which the economic practices of creating wealth, exchanging goods and services in markets, working for business corporations, and making profits are consistent with and practically supportive of a common good of society that stands beyond private goods and interests.

Christian Vocation in a Global Civil Society

Christians are called to glorify God and serve the good of the neighbor. This classic statement of vocational and social calling is deeply embedded within our Christian theological traditions—Roman Catholic (e.g., the Thomistic common good tradition), Lutheran, Calvinist. This fundamental vocational imperative is applicable to the contemporary business corporation. Within today's global society, this vocation should (1) aim at the common good—the good of the global community as a whole, which includes human society and all of creation, understood as the whole of the created order of nature; and (2) include the responsibility to participate in and support social institutions (political, economic, civic, family) that attempt, to our best human efforts and knowledge, to approximate with justice this larger good. This vocation is also appropriately colored by our acknowledgment of sin, and of the flawed nature of human knowledge and all historical social achievements. Thus, it also can appropriately require acts of criticism and even condemnation that denounce actions, practices, and institutional arrangements that violate or in some way fall short of our vision of the good, through discrimination, violations of human dignity, or other forms of injustice.

Within the current historical period, the integrated global society into which we are evolving is increasingly pluralistic and decentralized. We are moving away from the statist hierarchies of the late-nineteenth and twentieth centuries in which strongly activist government, whether democratic or nondemocratic, was assumed to be capable of ordering and actively managing much, if not all, of society. Now, our social institutions are becoming more pluralistic, with each sphere given more relative autonomy to achieve its respective task. Power is more decentralized, being dispersed more "from center to periphery." For instance, prior to World War I, the dominant nations of Europe, with their systems of global colonial rule, controlled most of the world's industrial strength. At the end of World War II, the economy of the United States comprised roughly 50 percent of the world's industrial output. That figure has dropped to approximately 25 percent, even though our own gross domestic product (GDP) has increased more than three-fold at the same time. These trends indicate fundamental shifts in the ways societies use power and control and have implications for how we can define and seek to institutionalize a "common good." Not only will governments have less unilateral power to define and promulgate a "common good" within a single society, but powerful nations such as the United States will also have less power to do so within the community of nations. The result will be more pluralistic, collaborative efforts, both across institutional sectors within a society as well as among the community of nations, both rich and poor. Indeed, the European powers who once carved up the world now call themselves the European Union, and North America's three economies are now bound by NAFTA, as mentioned earlier. These types of regional linkages will likely proliferate, as will global ones.

Within the global economy, pursuing the common good must be realized across nation-states throughout the community of nations. This includes the moral expectation that economic life, in the form of global market capitalism, rightly ordered, will demonstrate its capacity to move *most* people and nations out of poverty and dependence to achieve at least moderate levels of material well-being. I understand this moral expectation or "middle axiom" imperative for global capitalism to be a contemporary embodiment of the biblical mandate that the poor and disadvantaged should be treated justly and humanely, and not ignored or oppressed, by the larger community, and especially by the powerful within the community. Today, this larger community is the community of nations in its virtual totality as we shift toward an ever-more integrated and complex set of market-based relationships that are pulling nations and regions together not only economically, but also culturally and in some cases even politically (e.g., the European Union). In a market economy, the most powerful social actors will include business corporations in the private sector, which must therefore be included within the scope of this mandate of moral responsibility. This trend toward integration is not to deny the many instances of regional strife, as ethnic groups seek self-assertion at the expense of neighbors around them, e.g., the former Yugoslavia, and ethnic tensions in some parts of the former Soviet Union. But these will likely be exceptions to the larger trend toward integration.

I emphasize "*most* people and nations" because the twentieth century has taught us that no systems of wealth creation and no social engineering mechanisms that redistribute wealth seem capable of eliminating poverty or income and wealth inequalities altogether. It may be that our great-grandchildren will visit museums to see displays of what poverty was like once, just as we go to study primitive cultures; but we must recall that the very system whose ideological inspiration and telos was said to be the complete elimination of material poverty and inequality—Marxist-inspired centrally planned economies—has collapsed from within, rejected by virtually all those it was meant to serve. Yet it may be true that in one form or another, the saying of Jesus, "The poor you will always have with you," tells a tragic truth. The historical evidence demonstrates that societies whose economies have strongly established and legally protected market institutions (e.g., private property, competition, economic freedom) have served the poor far better than centrally planned economies by bringing most of its participants out of poverty to experience higher levels of material prosperity; that process has also typically been one characterized by high levels of inequality in wealth and income (cf. Berger, 1986). Hence, our moral expectations of business corporations in a global economy must be tempered by acknowledgment of what seems to be an empirical "given." Inequality of wealth and income will not disappear completely, either within nations or among nations. Realistically, not every less developed nation will reach the status of "fully developed" in the way that the United States currently exhibits. Nor will all those nations that do experience significant economic development be able to bring all of their citizens out of poverty into lifestyles that resemble those of the middle classes in industrialized countries. Rather, the open moral debate and challenge will be incremental: How many people globally should we expect the system of global market capitalism to bring out of poverty, in what countries, over what time frames, and as a result of what legal frameworks and political and economic strategies? What gains will count as extraordinary, good enough, inadequate, or utterly unacceptable? What beneficial impacts (material, economic, political, and cultural) do we wish markets and corporations to have on the societies in which they do business? In one sense, therefore, the key moral challenge for business corporations will be whether or not they can serve as the primary "engines of growth" that bring most poor people out of poverty. In reality, this situation is of course complicated. Business corporations cannot flourish without appropriate macroeconomic conditions in place—largely the responsibility of governments, through their own monetary and fiscal policies and systems of regulatory infrastructure, and more broadly by the protocols, rules, and regulatory frameworks created by multilateral institutions such as the World Bank, International Monetary Fund, and World Trade Organization.

As noted above, the thrust of my argument seems to put me in conflict with some Christian thinkers who argue that economic growth is morally problematic at best, and evil at worst (cf. Meeks, 1989; Daly and Cobb, 1989). But the moral slogan proposed by some that "less is better" is probably false. On the contrary, we must assert that "more is better" and "less is worse" as already hinted. This is not to deny that economic injustice can show its face vividly and dramatically within economic structures, practices, and assertions of wealth and power. Nor is it to deny that current patterns of economic distribution do not benefit substantial portions of the human population around the globe. Nor to suggest that all types of economic consumption are conducive to the moral life or the good society. Nor to deny the dangers of economic imperialism, that is, economic rationality and pursuits permeating into areas of social life where it is not appropriate. Nor to ignore the real challenges of pursuing economic growth in ways that respect the limits of nature and the demand for sustainable ecosystems. The global market economy is not without its problems; its challenges are immense. But it is to argue that world economic output must increase, rather than remain stagnant or decrease, if the problem of poverty is to be substantially alleviated. In other words, we must create more wealth globally, not less. Practically speaking, this means that business corporations, undergirded by the systems of institutional rules, cultural norms, religious ethics, and conditions that support them, must face the social, and indeed moral, challenges to be even more effective in producing goods and services in a broad-based way around the globe.

This proposition rejects some alternative strategies for global economic well-being, for instance that we could alleviate poverty *primarily* through nonmarket, redistributive mechanisms requiring fundamental systemic restructuring of global economic relationships, or that we could attempt to generate ecologically sustainable living by a radical shift away from an integrated global economy to smaller, regional and even highly localized self-contained economic interactions. The former have been tried and repudiated; the latter are likely to result in dramatic declines in standards of living around the globe.

An important question of corporate moral responsibility is the extent to which we should hold business corporations accountable to criteria of productive justice as well as of commutative and distributive justice. The idea of commutative justice dates to classical Greek philosophers such as Aristotle and has often been employed within theological ethics; it involves fairness in economic exchange and the formation of contracts. Distributive justice concerns the fair or equitable distributions of economic goods and services. It is to this latter form of justice that Christian ethics has devoted most of its energies in the field of economic ethics, often to the deep neglect of issues of production within economic life. But by productive justice I mean those qualities of character and those structural enablements in society that are necessary for effective productive activity—e.g., effort and hard work; professional and occupational disciplines and skills; legal codes and moral habits that both protect the human rights of all and secure responsible patterns of property, ownership, accountability, and due reward. While these will find expression in the enforcement mechanisms of a society, they are transmitted primarily within and by a culture's ethos.

Although the concept of productive justice is not well developed within twentieth-century Christian ethics, it has deep roots and it appears in the thought of John A. Ryan, an early-twentieth-century North American Roman Catholic ethicist. Ryan's work may constitute the most comprehensive, systematic, and detailed evaluation of a capitalist economic system within the field of Christian ethics, certainly within North America (cf. 1906, 1935, 1942). And while the idea is not clearly differentiated from classical Aristotelian-Thomistic concepts of justice, notions of productive justice emerge within Ryan's six "canons of distributive justice"—equality, needs, efforts and sacrifices, productivity, scarcity, and human welfare (1942). Under current conditions, it is likely that the notion of productive justice needs further elaboration and perhaps independent status.

This consideration of both productive and distributive justice begs the larger question of which social institutions we think are best responsible for the production of a society's wealth and which for its just distribution. Within a global market economy, business corporations operating within competitive markets will be both the primary producers and distributors of society's wealth and income. Yet governments also function in both areas. At the level of production, government creates and administers the "rules of the game" that properly seek to create a "level playing field" of commutative or exchange justice among producers. For instance, government aims to protect against monopoly and fraud, which could create unfair advantages among producers or cause harm to consumers. Earlier in this century, elaborate legal structures for "labor relations" were developed. More recently, we have instituted government mechanisms which aim to eliminate and even rectify past patterns of discrimination in the workplace. One can argue that these government interventions have implications for productive justice, even though they are essentially focused on just contract negotiations between management and workers, and thus are closer to what the classical tradition has called commutative justice. They seek to create a level, nondiscriminatory playing field within the workplace which will prevent some (unjust) economic inequalities of hiring and firing from occurring (thus eliminating the need for some eventual ameliorative government redistributive mechanisms).

At the level of distribution, governments make various efforts to change the distributional outcomes of the economic process, some direct, but most indirect. One direct measure is the federal minimum wage law, which demands that all producers pay workers no less than a certain wage. Most government interventions in distribution, though, are less direct. They do not intervene directly in the free price mechanism of markets, but merely react to the economic outcomes of that process. Progressive income taxes and various income subsidy programs are prime examples of political mechanisms intended to redistribute income, usually from the wealthy to the less wealthy. Inheritance taxes are a primary mechanism by which we both protect, but also redistribute, intergenerational social wealth.

Holding business corporations accountable for satisfying some criteria of distributive justice and/or distributional outcomes in a global economy will be very illusive, if not even counterproductive to social well-being and the common good. To do so implies that corporations have the capacity to manipulate the price they pay for labor in ways that may diverge substantially from the relatively free movement of prices in competitive labor markets. Rather, to the extent that we have attempted to change market-based distributions of wealth and income, we have done so through government mechanisms, the results of which have been varied and subject to public debate. In a more extensively global market economy, even the efficacy of government redistributive efforts may be subject to even greater scrutiny (and doubt) as the power of any single nation-state government acting unilaterally will become more limited in its capacity to influence the behavior of global markets, be they for labor, capital, or goods and services. To the extent that we do pursue matters of distributive justice, this will be more the realm of public policy than corporate policy; and procedures for commutative justice are likely to be taken up in highly negotiated and technical international agreements and supervised by such organizations as the World Trade Organization. In a global market economy, we may find it necessary to focus at least some of our moral attention with regard to business corporations on criteria of productive justice rather than limiting our focus to distributive or commutative justice.

By way of illustration, let us consider the issue of corporate executive compensation in relation to notions of justice. Many have argued that senior corporate executives, especially chief executive officers of some large U.S. corporations, receive too much compensation, which can come in the form of salary and benefits as well as bonuses and stock options. Indeed, senior corporate executives in the U.S. tend to receive proportionately higher compensation in relation to that of employees than do their counterparts in Europe and Japan. Upon what ethical grounds might we argue that such executives receive inappropriately high compensation? Some have argued intuitively on grounds of distributive justice that income inequalities that reach a certain ratio from highest paid to lowest paid worker in an organization become unjust. It is not clear what that ratio ought to be, but the point of the argument is that beyond some determinable threshold ratio, income inequalities intuitively become unjust. Some conclude, therefore, that corporations voluntarily, or even governments through regulations, should institute limits on how high that ratio should be.

But the argument here is primarily one of distributive justice, based not upon measurements of productivity—on the calculation of what time, energy, education, and focused cultivations have been invested in one person as compared to another, or on the probable, long-term contributions to the good of the civil society—but upon an intuitive judgment that certain unequal distributions of income are inherently unjust. On the other hand, others argue on the grounds of productivity that such high levels of compensation are unjust. Can the value and productivity of one person's contribution be equivalent to that of five hundred others in the organization? In other areas such as democratic elections, where one person equals one vote, we speak of justice as equality. But here we seem to say justice is five hundred salaries for some and one salary for another.

It is surely true that some executives do not help their corporations five hundred times more than other kinds of workers; some "rip off" their corporations, and waste their talents and economic gains. These examples are not morally defensible and sometimes not legal. Nevertheless, it may be a fact that some people are worth five hundred times more than others within a corporation. It may be easy to find five hundred people to take one job and do it well; it may be difficult to find one person in five hundred to do another. Often, the capacities of one person to form and sustain a corporation will mean a valued product or service for five thousand or even five million customers, and thus employment possibilities for five hundred or more workers. And the capacity to organize, coordinate, and evoke commitment to a common enterprise of five hundred or more people over time may have a cumulative effect in civil society that is worth more to the common good than what one worker, diligent and competent as he or she may be, who basically organizes only his or her own life. It may well transform a region, a community, or a great number of families from dependency and poverty to productivity and participation in the wider patterns of the culture. In other words, executive compensation often is not tied to the right kinds of incentives and measurements of productivity and corporate benefit. Should such compensation be tied more directly to the value of corporate equity (e.g., the stock price)? And if so, over what time periods, short or long term? Or to other measures of corporate well-being such as market share or even to measures of social well-being, such as worker safety, workplace diversity, or environmental protection? Should compensation be primarily in the form of cash or should it include major offerings of company equity? Indeed, corporate boards of directors continue to wrestle with the challenge of determining what performance measures to use in rewarding their senior executives, and in such wrestlings is the recognition that something more is at stake than the simplistic view that a free market determines just price. Issues of productive justice are behind these issues.

In light of these considerations, we are left with the question of how the ethical notion of productive justice, understood within a transformative theological framework, would view issues of executive compensation. Fundamentally, levels of compensation would be based upon measures of productivity and benefit for the organization, and indeed even upon measures of benefit for the larger society (the common good). Levels of compensation for senior executives would take into account their impacts on those within the organization. Would certain levels of compensation cause deep animosity within the organization, impeding the productivity of a large portion of its members?

I am reminded of a fiscal quarter in the early 1980s when General Motors announced large bonuses for its top executives; at the same time, its earnings were down and the company announced plant closings and large layoffs among rank-and-file workers. Not only did one wonder whether those large bonuses had any relation to organizational productivity, but one also was struck by the very predictable backlash and resentment within the organization, especially among the union workers. For many inside and outside the company, the perception was that senior executives were not willing to share the pain of financial difficulties and organizational downsizing. In other words, some levels of compensation could be judged inordinate, either because they are not based upon adequate measures of productivity and benefit and/or because they generate harmful consequences upon the productivity of others within the organization.

Furthermore, the transformationist position can also inform and shape the motives and intentions of senior executives. A transformationist would be motivated to "make a difference" within the organization and the larger society. Hence, one's motives would not be narrowly self-interested but drawn to the larger good that one contributes to one's organization (e.g., productivity) and even to society and humanity as a whole. Such an orientation toward service would less likely be driven by motivation for higher levels of financial remuneration than by other benefits or outcomes that result from one's position. Hence, a "transformationist" organization might be characterized by less disparity of compensation between the highest and lowest paid, although translating this inference into a more quantitative formula is illusive.

Even though questions of distributive justice will remain as an issue for governments, they are likely to become increasingly difficult for business corporations to address. Yet, we can return to the question of how criteria of productive justice might address the problem of poverty in the world today. How we define poverty and material well-being is, of course, an issue of considerable debate that raises fundamental questions of normative understanding (What constitutes the human? What is the good society?) as well as empirical measurement (What are the empirical measurements of poverty and human well-being and how precise can we be in their application?). If we focus, however, on the moral imperative to alleviate absolute poverty rather than on the regulation of relative poverty, we turn, in accord with the biblical imperative of doing justice toward the poor, toward those who are extremely vulnerable. Here we should note the challenge of measurability—we are likely to achieve more agreement on a definition of absolute poverty than relative poverty. For instance, the absence of poverty would at least include a nutritional diet that avoids malnourishment and would also include some basic quality of life indicators, such as reductions of infant mortality, increased life expectancy, improvements in access to health care, increased access to clean water and sanitation, decreasing fertility rates, and increasing levels of education.

To meet this problem without having the population become dependent requires their participation in productivity, the generating of wealth, a process that surely requires capital, management skills, market knowledge, accounting procedures, etc. It also requires a social context in which those who have, and are willing to share these things, can also become beneficiaries of the process of generating wealth for all concerned. But whether the social process of generating wealth that results in reductions in poverty is best accompanied by higher or lower levels of income and wealth inequality, and over what time period, is a moral and empirical question that should be left open to healthy debate and experimentation. The larger challenge is whether societies around the globe, through their governments and private sectors, can encourage the conditions in which the resources and the people can be brought together so that the bulk of the people have a chance to rise out of absolute poverty into tolerable levels of material well-being that permit individual flourishing and communal well-being, even if that means degrees of relative discrepancy of wealth and reward.

Wealth in Service of the Common Good

A theologically informed vision of global civil society provides the larger social and ecological framework within which to construct an ethic for the modern business corporation. It differs from the standard "secular" vision of the business corporation's purpose in society, characterized as follows: Business corporations exist solely to generate wealth by maximizing profits for owners while obeying all relevant laws. This standard view, for instance as espoused by Milton Friedman (cf. 1962, 1979), need not be a simplistic, short-termist profit-maximizing view of the world. It is enshrined in law (e.g., the fiduciary duty of managers to advance the interests of owners; legal protection of private property) and respects law (cf. also Hayek, 1973, 1976, 1979). It can justify the corporate pursuit of moral interests other than profits, but only instrumentally and/or if they are unavoidable restraints on profit-seeking. For instance, it would justify costs of environmental protection if and only if a cost-benefit analysis suggests that such an expenditure is efficient, likely to minimize costs and maximize profits over some longer time horizon. It also permits the pursuit of other moral goals by individuals, but merely as subjective private preferences which must be noncoercive and which are essentially beyond rational and objective scrutiny. For instance, individuals, as "principals," may wish to devote their own personal time or money to any number of "moral" causes they may freely choose. They may support religious associations or give their personal wealth to a charity or donate their compensation to their family or to a political party. But individuals may not do this in "agency" relationships such as management of publicly traded corporations, wherein they are called not to represent their own interests but the interests of the owners, which in a business corporation presumably is to generate or even to maximize profits.

Essentially, this standard minimalist vision of corporate purpose is secular, libertarian, and nonteleological. It begs the question of the good—either of particular moral ends that corporations should pursue other than profit maximization (or moral evils they should avoid) or of a larger common good to which they might contribute. These are, it is held, political goals to be pursued through legal channels and democratic governmental decision making, or questions of individual conscience and choice.

This minimalist libertarian vision is not entirely without merit; but if Christian ethics is to offer a fuller constructive ethic for the business corporation in a global market economy, it must take issue with this point of view. To a large extent, specifying norms, rules, and regulations about conduct within a business corporation—the stuff of ethics—will depend upon what we think is that organization's purpose. Different purposes require different rules and norms of conduct. If the sole purpose of a business corporation is to generate wealth by maximizing profit for owners, then certain ethical norms and rules will follow accordingly.

Christian ethics, working with a concept of productive justice, therefore, must become vigorously engaged in the ongoing public debate about the central question of the business corporation's proper purpose in society. In certain limited ways, it has done so throughout the twentieth century as industrialization, bureaucratization, technological change, and the rise of collectivism transformed society, but much of the focus was on political rather than economic life. In any case, it must do so anew as we enter the twenty-first century. But we shall now have to take up issues such as profits quite directly.

Of course, we might identify various circumstances in which profits are unethically obtained because of harms caused to certain parties in the course of a corporation's business (e.g., environmental laws are not adhered to, workers are discriminated against, customers are cheated, taxes are underpaid due to accounting irregularities or fraud), but we cannot do away with profits as one essential moral measuring stick for judging a corporation's value to society. Profits serve as a vital moral measure of the fiduciary stewardship of managers and employees to owners by measuring their efficiency in allocating scarce resources to effectively meet consumer demands. The condition of profitability serves as a means to disperse financial risk within society. If we have learned anything from the collapse of socialism, it is that other systems of capital allocation and risk management, namely public sector centralized planning, usually do not effectively manage one of society's most scarce resources—its financial capital—toward the end of efficiently satisfying society's material needs. And they seemed to establish equal or greater disparities of wealth and privilege in society. Practically speaking, there is no primary systemic alternative to private capital, and thus to the institution of profits. All known alternatives seem to lead to worse evils when they dominate or eliminate or obscure the role of private capital.

This is not to deny that public sources of capital cannot also be effective in some circumstances. Indeed, considerable capital is allocated to municipal and state bond markets for the provision of important social functions (e.g., public works, utilities, education). The solution to profits "unethically acquired" is not the abolition of profits but the strengthening of legal rules, social constraints, and moral values that protect against abuses of corporate power and private capital and better guarantee a mutuality of corporate and larger social interests. Furthermore, profits are generally best pursued within an economic environment that promotes and legally protects competition, or at least does not actively discourage it. Thus, to morally affirm efficiency and profitability also entails that we must, to some extent, accept the fact that there will be winners and losers within competitive industries with ensuing levels of worker dislocation. We must morally embrace the dynamic empirical reality of what Joseph Schumpeter called capitalism's "creative destruction"—the relentlessly dynamic process whereby technological innovation, entrepreneurship, capital mobility, and organizational expertise make obsolete old products and production processes in favor of new ones (1954). Barring unfair rules or practices, we must generally accept the reality of losers (failing firms) for their inability to perform their function of allocating financial and human capital as effectively and efficiently as other competitors. This is not necessarily, though, to impute moral culpability or blame to every instance of business failure or significant profit loss in a dynamic and diverse competitive market economy. Business failure can be a "nonmoral" matter, due to changes in technological innovation, customer demand, or macroeconomic conditions that are unanticipated by even the most astute and knowledgeable entrepreneur or senior manager.

Freedom of initiative and also creativity, both expressed, for example, through entrepreneurship and technological innovation, must also be highly valued. We value them not merely for their instrumental value—because they contribute to the economic process and the financial success of business organizations; we also value them intrinsically—because they enable human activities that are "fundamentally human" and can be constitutive of personal growth and development and effective participation in society. Freedom of initiative and creativity in the economic sphere can serve as attributes of vocation and stewardship that enable both personal flourishing as well as effective service toward the neighbor and the common good. As I shall argue in the next section, these qualities become components of "productive justice" within a business organization. They may even be manifestations of the skills and abilities encouraged by Jesus in the parable of the talents in Matthew 25.

Indeed, the debate about business's proper purpose in society may best be shaped by the capacity of Christian theology to articulate a larger substantive vision of human life rightly ordered in society, according to which the moral expectations of business corporations and their managers and workers can be defined. We can ask, for example, what ends, purposes, standards, and expectations in addition to profitability can a Christian ethic advocate as appropriate to business. If profitability and competitiveness are affirmed as important and indeed necessary moral criteria for judging the performance of business corporations in a global economy, they cannot from a Christian ethical perspective be the only ones. They still beg essential questions of morality generally and of Christian morality specifically.

Can and how should we evaluate the goodness or badness of the goods and services that are produced, apart from the basic market mechanisms in which customers make personal moral judgments by deciding whether or not to purchase that good or service? What effects do business organizations have on the persons who work for them and should we be morally concerned with these impacts? What impacts do business corporations have on the larger communities in which they are located, both socially and ecologically? These are fundamental questions of the moral good which imply larger questions such as "What is the good person?" and "What is the good society?" and "What is the good earth?" Indeed, it is these larger questions about the content of the moral good that Christian faith and theology can provide some moral substance. And it is such content that can move us beyond the essentially secular, libertarian, minimalist vision of corporate purpose that dominates the world today.

If it is so that the basic purpose of economic life generally, and of business corporations specifically, should be to generate wealth for society in ways that are not only profitable but also serve the "common good" by contributing to the development of an ecologically sustainable global civil society, we can say that the "common good" should be universal and wholistic. We are faced with a massive magnification of the meaning of the term "common." Theologically, this universalism is grounded in the religious premise of the essential sacredness and equality of all human beings and in the claim that the only God worth worshiping is the Creator of the whole world. As such, we can assert no moral hierarchy that favors some individuals or nations over others in the pursuit of appropriate levels of material prosperity that permit the flourishing of global civil society. Wholistic perspectives are required because the moral good must encompass not only the human good but also the good of the whole earth, its ecosystems and its myriad of species. This is not to argue for a romantic view of naure, the essential equality of all species, or the "rights" of other species. Tom Derr has addressed these ideological temptations in the ecological movement (see his *Environmental Ethics and Christian Humanism*, volume 2 in this series). But it is to argue that the moral good extends beyond the good only of the human species because humans are responsible under God for the world given to us. As such, economic activities and the pursuit of global material prosperity must aim toward the long-term sustainability of the earth's ecosystems and future human generations. In the next section, therefore, we must turn our attention to the substantive ethical content and implications of this Christian vision of corporate purpose. In the meantime, we need to review several other approaches and raise the issue of "strategic discernment."

While advocating that a transformative ethic of conversion is the most practical and universalistic view for the new global economic context, I do not rule out other basic approaches. The global market economy is not so monolithic in its characteristics or its effects as to suggest that a transformative posture of constructive yet critical engagement is always optimally effective. There may be instances in which a society's economic institutions or practices are so unjust or evil as to prohibit effective participation, suggesting the appropriateness of alternative strategies such as prophetic denunciation or protest. For example, many people considered foreign direct investment in South Africa during its apartheid period to be such an instance. Indeed, even Rev. Leon Sullivan, Baptist pastor and member of General Motors' board of directors, and creator of the Sullivan Principles, eventually came to renounce his own principles as an ethically inadequate strategic response to apartheid. Defining minimum moral criteria for policy and practice by foreign multinationals with foreign direct investments in South Africa, their initial intent was clearly transformative. Sullivan's aim in the 1970s and 1980s was to make foreign direct investment into a constructive moral force for the gradual transformation (eradication) of the racist apartheid system. Hence, not only were multinational corporations to avoid any overt racial discrimination within their own business practices, but they were also charged to work constructively and strategically for the larger system's transformation. In other words, constructive engagement, adhering to minimal moral criteria of nondiscrimination, was initially embraced as a more effective means for change than economic disengagement and disinvestment from the South African economy.

These motifs can be seen as a creative practical contribution to the idea of productive justice. Eventually, though, ten years later, Sullivan urged a strategic "about-face," arguing that there was sufficient historical evidence to demonstrate this strategy's ineffectiveness in serving as a force for change in South Africa. By the mid-1980s, he had renounced his own principles and urged U.S. and other foreign multinational signatories of the Sullivan Principles to leave South Africa. While Rev. Sullivan's larger moral objective remained unchanged—the dismantling of an evil, unjust racist system—his strategy shifted radically. In his mind, that shift in strategy was necessary for the very sake of the larger moral objective. The patterns of commutative justice and distributive justice appeared to be so systematically violated that no attempt to preserve productive justice seemed viable. Ironically, South Africa's system of apartheid was peacefully and constitutionally dismantled within a few short years of Sullivan's renouncement of his own transformative strategy of constructive engagement. This relatively peaceful, nonviolent transition was no doubt due to several larger forces at work in the world and in South Africa, e.g., the collapse of Soviet communism, and the global financial community's unwillingness to provide foreign credit to the South African regime, but now the demand for productive justice has returned.

At the same time, many in the U.S. religious community and the larger global society had advocated strategic disengagement with South Africa long before Sullivan. Many U.S. religious groups, both denominations and religious orders, had been actively engaged in the divestment movement, advocating that U.S. corporations cease business operations in South Africa and withdrawing their investment in those corporations that did not respond favorably.

Deciding whether and how to participate economically with apartheid South Africa is a poignant example of the strategic discernment that must be an inherent component of a Christian ethic that is relevant to economic life and attempts to influence the activities of business corporations. All factions of the U.S. religious community were clear in their moral judgment of the apartheid regime and their final goal (its eventual dismantling). Apartheid violated fundamental theological assumptions about human dignity and human community. Their differences, though, were at the level of strategy—of the most effective means to accomplish that goal, and specifically, of the role that foreign business corporations should play in that larger moral drama.

Likewise, while we can argue generally for a transformative strategy of constructive engagement with business corporations in today's global economy, we acknowledge that other strategies can also sometimes be appropriate and defensible. For instance, we may believe a regime, institution, practice, or product to be so evil that its amelioration or elimination is necessary, and judge that to be most effectively possible through a strategy of nonparticipation or even active denunciation and disengagement. Are some political regimes so corrupt or evil that we should not engage in business relations with them? Or are some products so harmful that consumers should advocate boycotts or urge their illegality? Are there times when individuals could find a company's practices or products so reprehensible or harmful to make employment there unconscionable?

Such judgments might compel one to adopt a "Christ against culture" approach in such cases, advocating acts of prophetic denunciation. For instance, how should one treat the tobacco industry, which produces and distributes products inherently harmful to the user? Likewise, on a global basis, how ought we to engage ourselves economically with countries like China, whose government still condones practices in flagrant violation of fundamental human rights such as forced prison labor and the sometimes violent suppression of public debate of and dissent from government positions and uses of power. Some U.S. companies, for instance, have chosen not to enter or have withdrawn from Chinese markets due to objections to some Chinese government practices. Others have remained and more have entered those same markets, illustrating a diversity of strategic moral responses to a social environment containing some morally reprehensible practices. South Africa and China are but two time-bound examples of special cases that will continue to challenge Christians and others as we seek to discern strategic responses of economic involvement, conditional engagement, or avoidance with respect to those whose practices we find morally problematic.

At the other end of the strategic spectrum might there also be instances when we affirm a strategy more consistent with Niebuhr's "Christ of culture" approach? Without naively deifying any human achievements or making theology inordinately and dangerously immanent, are there not also contexts in which we might conclude that economic life or some business activities are tolerable approximations of our visions of God's intentions for the world and of Christian ethical norms?

Are there also occasions in economic life, albeit usually transitory and subject to change and moral decay, when historical reality seems to have been morally transformed by human effort to warrant a "Christ of culture" strategy? Are there times when we can say that Christian ethical norms are, rather effectively, embodied with an actual historical practice? Are there corporations, for instance, whose practices and/or products for the most part adequately reflect our best Christian ethical norms? If so, while eschewing an aura of triumphalism or moral imperialism, we might still affirm a strategy of accommodation and affirmation of these practices. For example, there may be examples of corporations whose products are judged beneficial to users and society and whose internal practices and external relationships are sufficiently exemplary according to legal standards and moral criteria (e.g., respect for human dignity, criteria of fairness and nondiscrimination, contributory to civil society, sensitivity to environmental well-being) such that we judge them to be morally exemplary models of economic excellence. In such cases, a strategic posture toward them would certainly not be prophetic denunciation or disengagement, nor even primarily conversionist, but more properly "defensive" or conservative in the sense that we would support and defend their institutional practices from threats to their existence or flourishing.

The transformational Christian ethic implied in Niebuhr's "Christ transforming culture," in other words, recognizes the strategic propriety of other positions—"Christ against culture" and "Christ of culture"—under certain conditions that must be carefully discerned. That is so precisely because, in many respects, Christ and culture remain in paradox, and Christ ordinarily is above culture. That is what makes it possible for Christ, the symbol of all theological ethics, to engage cultural realities transformationally.

Ethical Implications for Corporations in a Global Era

The general moral purpose for business, based on a transformative theological basis as discussed in the previous section, is to generate wealth in ways that are profitable and that serve the common good by contributing to the development of an ecologically sustainable global civil society. The major implications of that basic perspective for business corporations as they seek to fulfill that overarching vision in the particular context of a global economy involves at least the following four ethical criteria, in addition to the criteria of efficiency and profitability which are necessary to this arena of human activity: (1) that their products are beneficial and not intentionally harmful to users and society; (2) that in their relations with various constituent or stakeholder groups, they adhere to basic standards of productive justice, defined especially in terms of respect for human rights; (3) that they support appropriate countervailing institutions (e.g., democratic governments able to generate and enforce effective regulations, voluntary associations, cultural institutions, viable communities, etc.) whose combined efforts aim to create and sustain the well-functioning of civil society; and (4) that their activities do not inhibit or block long-term environmentally sustainable development.

Creating Products and Services that Avoid Harm
and Generate Benefit to Users and Society

The moral proposition that a company's products should be beneficial and not harmful to users and society assumes that societies can identify and agree to at least some minimal standards of human well-being. In this sense, a Christian ethical approach moves beyond libertarian or contractarian approaches that eschew efforts to define the good. This criterion is based upon respect for persons and a conviction in the essential and equal dignity of all persons. It can be seen as a partial institutional embodiment of Christian love insofar as it seeks negatively to avoid harms which impede the good of the neighbor. This is consistent with the way in which Luther and other reformers understood the Ten Commandments to be minimalist negative injunctions whose fuller ethical purpose was a positive, indeed radical, commitment to love the neighbor and seek his/her good.

Democratic, industrialized nations like the United States already have a complex web of well-developed social infrastructure that attempts to avoid or minimize some harmful outcomes generated from the production and distribution of economic goods and services. Layers of government legislation, with mandated regulatory agencies for enforcement, seek to protect various parties from various types of harm within the economic process, including workers, consumers, and the general public. Systems of criminal and civil law also serve as a means to protect or compensate parties from harm. Special interest groups, such as consumer advocacy groups, unions, and environmentalists, act as "countervailing powers" to business activities. These social forces, as well as the influences of education and religion, all combine to shape the ongoing public debate about what constitutes social harm as real and perceived threats change with changing products, data, perceptions, and anxieties.

As we come to the close of the most highly regulated century in modern history, it seems clear that although there may be a reduced role for government in some areas, the public debate about social harm is not undergoing a radical "sea change" or departure from what has preceded us. We are not departing from the general social expectation that business corporations should be dissuaded from certain activities that cause social harm. Nor that government, as well as other social institutions and influences, are appropriately charged to try to create the legal and social conditions to prevent or minimize social harms. What is subject to substantial debate is how such expectations are best embodied within concrete institutional forms in the midst of changing conditions. How much regulation can we expect from government agencies, after which their effectiveness is marginal or even negative? When is regulation more harmful than the harm it was meant to prevent? When is regulation merely an ideological smokescreen to protect a special interest at the unfair expense of the general interest? When do regulatory laws and agencies outlive their historical effectiveness due to changing circumstances? When does the cost of regulation outweigh its social benefit? How do we make judgments about harm when some social harms and benefits are so comingled that clarity at the level of social policy seems impossible? To what extent should we depend upon more paternalistic approaches to guard against social harm such as government regulation or upon individualistic strategies that focus on education and individual responsibility? As countries like the United States continue to shift away from heavy command-and-control government regulation of social activity to more flexible approaches, we are likely to see greater emphasis on consumer education and individual responsibility, as well as on liability laws that prompt corporations themselves to take greater efforts to avoid some of the harms that government regulations are eventually created to try to correct.

Within democratic societies that are pluralistic and increasingly global, as is ours, there is no single standard or definition of the human good that permits widespread consensus on what constitutes benefit and harm in all situations. This pluralism is no less true of Christian ethics than of the wider public. Even if such a widely shared standard or substantive vision existed, we would still be naive to assume that all social interests organically or easily converge to create a coherent vision of the common good. Sometimes, the interests of various constituent groups are inherently in conflict or at odds with another, suggesting that the common good is sometimes not so "common." This is due, in part, to the fact that our views of the world and our visions of the common good are at best insightful yet partial, and at worst sometimes perverse and corrupted by sin. Hence, discerning the good to be achieved and the bad to be avoided is itself the subject of ongoing reflection, conflict, and debate. Yet, such debates about benefit and harm can themselves be healthy and creative. It may even be that it is only through this sometimes conflictual, rough-and-tumble public debate that society's general interests—the common good—emerge and clarify themselves. The fact that we debate these matters suggests that a certain, if often vague, reasonability about the good is possible.

Minimally this criterion requires that corporations avoid producing goods and services that knowingly cause egregious harm to users and society, even in the absence of applicable laws or other external social constraints that would mitigate against such practices. Corporations become duty-bound to disclose information about potential risks and harms of their products to users, especially in situations or societies where such information may not be readily available to the end user. This becomes especially relevant when doing business in less developed countries whose consumers may lack general educational awareness or whose social infrastructure may lack appropriate countervailing institutions to protect against such types of harm. In effect, *caveat emptor*, "buyer beware," does not apply, or at least would be severely restricted in its application. Examples would include dangerous products without warning labels or sufficient instructions for proper use.

In effect, this criterion implies that "the market" is not always a sufficient "judge" of moral harm and benefit to consumers. While an educated consumerate may generally be a good measure of social harm and benefit in its ability to choose freely among products in a competitive marketplace, it is not always so, especially where harms may be hidden or only long-term or in the case of some consumers who may not be fully capable of making good choices (e.g., children). This criterion implies that companies must create appropriate procedures and tests that try to anticipate, as fully as existing technology and scientific knowledge will permit, how their products could cause short or long-term harm to users or society. With such a commitment, one wonders whether Ford Motor Company would have continued with production of the Pinto in the 1970s when it had projections for the number of deaths and injuries that would result from its exploding gas tank. Likewise, one wonders whether Dow Corning would have proceeded as long as it did with the manufacture and sale of silicone breast implants when evidence from users was mounting that severe and debilitating health problems were resulting from the implant. (Undoubtedly, we can also raise moral questions about the values of the larger culture that demands breast implants. While some women have obtained breast implants to correct deformities resulting from surgeries to remove life-threatening cancers, others have desired implants for purely cosmetic reasons. Larger normative questions of gender expectations and esteem are also at stake.)

On the other hand, one notes the example of Johnson & Johnson, which went to extraordinarily costly lengths not only to withdraw all Tylenol products from the market after the Tylenol poisoning incidents of several years ago, but also to cease producing the Tylenol caplets altogether, because they were more prone to tampering than other Tylenol products. Hence, corporations do well within their own corporate cultures to create policies, procedures, and opportunities for moral debate and practical reasoning whereby questions of harm and benefit to consumers and society are raised, deliberated internally, and adequately resolved within the production process. The goal is to anticipate potential harms from products and services, not only to avoid potentially expensive litigation and/or "negative press," which harms corporate image and reputation, but also for the well-being of consumers themselves. Indeed, in the long run, one hopes that this moral stance is generally "good for business," generating long-term trust from consumers and the general public. Hence, this criterion may also imply that a corporation has a duty to disclose its knowledge of potential harm to the general public and, where practical, even to advocate for appropriate regulations of a product among competitors within an industry group and/or with the appropriate governmental regulatory bodies.

Let us consider some harmful or potentially harmful products such as alcoholic beverages and tobacco products to see how this criterion might apply to corporations. While alcoholic beverages can be harmful when misused, they are not inherently harmful. When consumed in moderation by most adults, they may provide some benefits to the user, including nutrition. More often they provide culinary pleasure (good taste) and a desired mild euphoria. In some cases, the production of alcoholic beverages represents rich cultural heritages that provide character, local color, and pride to a geographic region (e.g., many beers and wines in Europe, as well as newly developing microbreweries in U.S. cities). Clearly, alcoholic consumption can be harmful when abused, not only to the physical health of the user but to others as well (e.g., innocent victims who are killed or injured by a drunk driver, families who suffer with alcoholics). But these harms are not inherent to the product and our social deliberation and judgment about alcoholic beverages is shaped and nuanced by a consideration of both benefits and harms to the user and society. Because we cannot unequivocally conclude that alcoholic beverages are harmful, we permit their production and consumption, but with various constraints and regulations aimed to minimize some harms. We restrict the purchase of alcoholic beverages through liquor licenses, and we prohibit their sale to minors. Local communities and even producers participate in educational campaigns that aim at responsible use of alcoholic beverages. In the case of alcohol, we conclude that producers are duty-bound not only to communicate the risks and harms of abusive consumption to users, but also actively to engage in creative social and community efforts to combat alcohol abuse and to work with governments to create and support appropriate regulation as well as cultural patterns of constrained use for the sake of the common good of society.

On the other hand, tobacco products provide a less ambiguous moral response, based upon a different balance of benefits and harms to users and society. Tobacco products are inherently harmful to users. When "taken as directed" they can cause physical harm and death. There seems to be no benign use of tobacco as there may be with alcoholic beverages. Tobacco products are more likely than alcohol to become addictive to the user. The negative costs of tobacco use are experienced not only by the user in the form of bad health and death but are passed on to others in society as well, such as employers and others who must assume some of the additional "costs" that smokers incur. These costs include higher health care expenses to insurers and less productivity to employers, in the form of greater absenteeism due to smoking-related illnesses. Indeed, the benefits of smoking to the user (a short-term physical "high" from tobacco ingested into the blood stream) seem grossly outweighed by the harms, both to the user and to society.

It comes as no surprise, therefore, that tobacco production and consumption is even more highly regulated than alcoholic beverages. In the United States, government regulation prohibits sales to minors, requires warning labels on all packages, and prohibits television ads. In the face of steadily increasing public opinion against cigarette smoking domestically, tobacco companies devote growing sums of money to public relations campaigns to protect smokers' rights, to lobbyists and political action committees to influence the legislative process, and for legal expenditures that attempt both to defend against the lawsuits of plaintiffs against the companies as well as to file law suits against some state and local governments whose regulations provide even further restrictions or constraints on smoking. In spite of harms to users and society, tobacco products are not illegal in the United States, based to a large extent upon our society's basic moral affirmation of individual rights and the legal protection of such activity construed as an individual right guaranteed by the Constitution. Many would find a blanket legal prohibition of smoking to be excessively paternalistic (and a violation of constitutional rights), and would argue that the inevitable emergence of a black market would create new social problems. People have a right to take certain risks, and public policy cannot force everyone to avoid every bad risk.

Even though a blanket legal prohibition of cigarette smoking is socially problematic and thus not advisable by most, one is still left with the question of whether a theologically based transformationist position could advocate personal participation in the tobacco industry. At moral issue is the question of whether one could find a compelling argument to justify contributing to the production of a product that is inherently harmful to the user. Could the individual Christian conclude that the many positive social benefits that accrue from the tobacco industry (e.g., jobs, tax revenues), or even to the individual worker (primarily in the form of personal employment) be sufficient to offset the fact that one's product is harmful to the health of the user, sometimes fatally so? I believe the answer would generally be negative. The Christian worker, seeking to advance the good of the neighbor and society through one's vocation at work, would find that the prima facie mandate not to harm would create a moral presumption against producing a product that is inherently harmful to users. Instead, the Christian would be compelled to seek some other work that produces a product that avoids such harm to users. Likewise, one would conclude that a business corporation itself, seeking to adhere to the moral criterion of avoiding harm, could not advocate entry into the tobacco industry. For instance, it seems unimaginable that a company like Johnson & Johnson, which places respect for public health and safety as its number one corporate goal, could ever consider entering the tobacco business, even apart from the obvious fact that there may be few synergies (e.g., common technologies, product lines, overlapping marketing strategies, or production processes that could create more efficient or profitable business practices) between the health products industry and the tobacco industry.

Ethical issues arise regarding the moral appropriateness of U.S. tobacco companies' aggressive expansion into new global markets, notably formerly socialist as well as emerging growth countries in the former Third World. In the face of weak or nonexistent governmental regulations in most foreign markets, should we expect U.S. tobacco companies voluntarily to refrain from certain practices (e.g., in advertising, warning labels, sales to minors) that are prohibited in the United States? I would argue usually yes, not because there is any inherent moral duty to adhere to U.S. standards abroad, but because our standards aim to limit some harms of tobacco consumption. If such regulations are effective in limiting or avoiding some harms in this country, producers generally should adhere to such regulations abroad as well, as a means to adhere to the general criterion to avoid harm and create benefit to users. Yet, the moral appropriateness of these restraints on tobacco sales abroad are all undercut by the deeper contradiction that tobacco production and consumption pose to the larger moral demand that products and services avoid harm and contribute to the well-being of the user and the larger society. Finally, we seem to tolerate a highly regulated tobacco industry as a less harmful solution than an unregulated one or an outright legal prohibition, which infringes upon personal freedoms and arguably constitutional rights.

The mandate of avoiding harm and benefiting the user and society also implies restrictions on the ways that products and services are marketed and advertised. For instance, advertising that flagrantly objectified persons as sex objects is arguably harmful for its portrayal of men and women in unhealthy ways. Some consumer product ads portray the "good guy" as a person who always breaks social convention. But is it always "party time" for the good person, or the good society? Likewise, ads that inordinately glorify violence are inconsistent with a deeper Christian vision of God's intentions for humane and nonviolent human relationships. Hence, qualities such as sexism, racism, violence, and inordinate or crass materialism are inconsistent with the moral demand to avoid harm. How we define these "isms" and exactly where we "draw the moral line in the sand" with respect to our tolerance and permissibility levels is often illusive and variable. And, within a pluralistic society that tolerates and indeed celebrates freedom of speech and expression as a positive social value, we find some portrayals morally questionable and problematic, yet do not wish to prohibit their expression. A transformative ethic would not always equate the morally permissible with the morally ideal, nor the ethical with the legally enforceable.

In addition to the avoidance of harm, this criterion would call for unified, standardized health and safety norms and regulations that can be applied uniformly across nation-states. The first sign of a trend in this direction is partially a function of global internationalization and integration. I have in mind the trends in standardization of regulations within the European Union, certain provisions in the NAFTA legislation, and the public outrage at working conditions in some manufacturing plants in underdeveloped regions. The more these become policy, they may drive up some costs of production precisely as they facilitate transnational development. Exceptions would be where trends toward uniformity mask or ignore important, morally relevant cultural differences such as some religious norms and practices. Beyond the minimal duty to avoid harm and the higher mandate to treat all others as neighbors, this criterion affirms a growing commitment to higher levels of quality and customer satisfaction, especially among firms that are experiencing heightened levels of global competition. It is also consistent with emergent efforts to create universal standards and measures of quality.

Adhering to Basic Standards of Productive Justice

Adherence to basic standards of justice affirms not only the dignity of persons but also acknowledges the sociality of human nature and of human fulfillment. Individuals develop, flourish, and best serve the neighbor within social and institutional arrangements that respect basic conditions of justice. Within economic life, organizational as well as individual effectiveness can be enhanced by realizing conditions of justice within the fabric of organizational structures and cultures. I include moral notions that emphasize both individuality as well as sociality—the value of the individual as well as the value of community. Hence, with respect to the individual, justice must include such notions as honoring contracts, honesty, respect for human rights, and non-discrimination, as well as personal traits such as personal initiative, creativity, risk-taking, and hard work. With respect to the communal dimension of human fulfillment, justice must embrace such notions as teamwork and trust.

66

Together, these standards and qualities function to create important conditions of "productive justice." These concepts of justice and personal characteristics help enable individuals and organizations to produce goods and provide services effectively in a rapidly changing global economy.

This linkage between productive effectiveness and justice is important from a Christian perspective and is vital to a transformationist ethic in a global market economy. Not only does it invoke the theologically grounded argument that morally affirms the wealth-creating purpose of business corporations, but it argues that this purpose is best accomplished within a moral fabric of just relationships in the work organization. Hence, this criterion rubs against the grain of two propositions embedded within the "conventional wisdom" of much Christian ethical analysis of business and economic life: (1) that the basic private sector objective of producing goods and providing services (generating social wealth) is itself morally dubious and suspect, if not evil; and (2) that corporations best pursue that objective according to rules, norms, and practices that are themselves unjust or ethically suspect. In other words, both the ends and means of business activity have received strong moral criticism from much of the tradition of Christian ethics. On the contrary, the transformational position affirms the potential goodness of the business enterprise itself and boldly proposes that, over time, productive efficacy is best advanced through the practice of justice.

In this context, it is important to reaffirm what has already been treated. The conception of "productive justice" advocated here seeks to articulate those personal qualities and institutional relationships that optimize production of wealth in service to society, and to supplement the already well developed concepts of "distributive justice" and "commutative justice" discussed in the previous section. Productive justice is that form of justice particularly appropriate to economic life and more specifically to the formation of persons and institutional relationships that shape the fabric of the business organization.

To the chagrin of some, this places one dimension of justice, at least partially yet fittingly, in the service of the pursuit of wealth and profitability. It seeks to articulate the appropriate moral means or conditions for the creation of goods and services within work organizations. This does not imply that all notions or conditions of justice in a society should be fully subservient to economic production, or that justice is only important to the creation of economic goods. It would be unjust if a university falsified learning or a hospital sacrificed healing only for some economic end; but it is unjust to expect a business corporation not to pursue this end and only to pursue learning or healing. Sufficient production of material goods and services is not the only goal of a good society. Thus, a theory of justice for the whole of civil society requires moral demands other than those covered under productive justice. Indeed, larger demands of social justice can and do stand in conflict with unlimited production of material goods and services. Yet our intent here is not a comprehensive articulation of all aspects of social justice, but more modestly to articulate the conditions of "productive justice" that should best guide economic organizations as they produce goods and services.

Some principles that overarch all areas of human activity, however, remain pertinent to productive justice. Honesty is required in universities, courts of law, medical centers, and family life; and so it is in business. The honoring of contracts entails a rejection of bribery, deception, and corruption. In a rapidly changing economy, honesty also implies the need for organizations to be more careful and cautious about the promises or "psychological contracts" they make with employees regarding terms of employment. Major trends such as technological change and globalization quicken the pace of "creative destruction" within the workplace, making workers' skills and work-group obsolescence a greater threat than in the past. This dynamism puts long-term employee relationships at risk and makes ongoing commitment to worker training and retraining on the part of both organization and employee even more critical than in the past.

Respect for human rights within the workplace affirms the general moral conviction that all persons deserve certain minimal levels of treatment independent of social position. This includes the expectation that economic choices are rightly free and uncoerced, as in decisions about employment and purchasing. This implies a rejection of all coerced labor, including such practices as slave labor and child labor, which are contrary to human dignity and development. Such respect also affirms the right to safe and clean working conditions as well as the right to organize labor unions. It supports the payment of a "living wage" that provides a level of livelihood that sustains at least the minimal material conditions for decent human life. Anything less constitutes "slave labor" in the sense that it fails to satisfy minimal conditions of human dignity. Yet the payment of a living wage can be unrealistic unless economies can expand at rates higher than population growth rates, and can do so in ways that are ecologically sustainable in the long run.

How these expectations get embodied within business practice in a global economy is not always easily discerned. While they tend to be well-institutionalized within the legal and social infrastructures of most industrialized nations, they often are not in less developed nations. This gap creates special challenges for global corporations doing business in such societies as they struggle to determine whether and how they might implement ethical standards that exceed local laws, customs, and accepted practices, or that might incur additional business expenses that threaten to place corporations at competitive disadvantage in a particular marketplace.

The transformationist stance, though, would compel corporations to try "to make a difference" by raising such standards and conditions higher than the surrounding area if prevailing conditions are judged morally deficient. Hence, even in the face of widespread local use of child labor, the global corporation would be compelled to take all reasonable measures to find ways to eliminate or overcome this practice within its own labor practices. It would make strong efforts to provide sufficient compensation for dignified human life for all its employees, in some cases with predictable implications for productivity and training.

Nondiscrimination includes a commitment to equality of opportunity and treatment within the workplace irrespective of gender or race. Forms of discrimination that are racist or sexist would be rejected, based on the moral premise that God created all humans fundamentally equal. To consider a concrete example in practice, this criterion affirms the ideal of eliminating sexism in the workplace, even in parts of the world where men's and women's roles are still traditionally ordered, resulting in severe restrictions on women's access to professional and occupational roles and advancement.

Productive justice also affirms personal traits conducive to high productivity and performance within work organizations. These include capacities for teamwork and such qualities as hard work, effort, initiative, and seriousness of purpose. To argue for them as aspects of productive justice is to claim them as qualities worthy of reward within the workplace. Individuals who make superior contributions to the effectiveness of their organizations may deserve higher rewards than others who do not. I am not suggesting productivity as the *only* morally relevant factor in providing organizational rewards. It is usually balanced by other factors and considerations, such as seniority, race, and gender, and other difficult-to-quantify fairness considerations within the unique cultures of business organizations. Nor am I suggesting that monetary compensation and organizational status and power should be the sole or primary motivators for Christians or others to function within the workplace. But I am suggesting that high productivity, generally, with the personal qualities instrumental to its flourishing, can function as "virtues" to be supported and rewarded within today's global market economy. This is true because business organizations function today with higher levels of institutional insecurity based upon the rapid pace of economic change, making highly productive workers even more essential to their own survival and health. It is also true if we are to infuse business corporations with the larger moral goal of serving as the global economy's engine of sustainable development, especially within less developed countries.

Affirming personal traits conducive to high levels of productivity and performance also implies an obligation of work organizations to make appropriate and continuing investments in their workers, to create and enhance the conditions necessary for workers to survive and flourish as productive contributors to the organization. Hence, on-going worker training and education, as well as team-building efforts, become a vital dimension of productive justice.

Adherence to standards of productive justice within the business corporation is an important condition for the development of global civil society. These standards acknowledge that the moral goods that business corporations rightly seek are not merely instrumental (primarily material wealth and the generation of profits) but also can be intrinsic and associational. John Paul II asserts, "the purpose of a business firm is not simply to make a profit, but is to be found in its very existence as a community of persons who in various ways are endeavoring to satisfy their basic needs, and who form a particular group at the service of the whole of society" (1991, #35). In other words, the good corporation is judged not merely by the value of its material outputs for social well-being but also by the quality and justice of its internal and external relationships. It can be measured as well by the extent to which it provides opportunities for human interaction, association, and community that permit human development and flourishing. Hence, while the purpose of business corporations is primarily material and instrumental, neither is it devoid of ethical content and character. It should seek to satisfy basic conditions of productive justice as it pursues its economic purpose.

Supporting the Development of Appropriate Countervailing Institutions

Creating a global civil society cannot depend exclusively upon business corporations, but rather results from the effective functioning of institutions from the several sectors of society: familial, political, legal, economic, religious, and cultural. The institutions of these various sectors include not only those of democratic government, which provides a legal framework for economic life, including its regulatory functions; but also a myriad of independent organizations, including those designed for education, philanthropy, social services, media, labor solidarity, professional development, and special interest advocacy (for example, on behalf of groups as such as children, the elderly, and the disabled). In a well-functioning pluralistic society, these sectors combine to serve as effective "counter-balances" against the tendency for any one sector to assert inordinate power in society. Productive business corporations create many of the conditions for the flourishing of civic society, and through their effective generation of wealth make others possible. At the same time, well-functioning democratic governments and a vibrant array of other sector organizations create a context in which business can work, and also form competent people who are able to be creative in their economic activity. Together, they serve as countervailing powers interacting to create some semblance of a "common good" for society.

Hence, our goal is not merely the creation and nurturing of well-functioning corporations, for even highly successful corporations can become a threat to the larger well-being of society if their power is unrestrained by other values, cultural forces, laws, and social institutions. Unrestrained will-to-power eventually and inevitably leads to evil consequences. Within economic life, unchecked market power can lead to the inordinate commodification of meaning and values. Economic rationality and activity can be good within its own sphere and proper limits, yet can be dehumanizing, debasing, and corrupting beyond its proper sphere. Rather, our goal is the creation of flourishing business corporations within a fertile social context that not only restrains the inevitable opportunities to abuse their power and influence within society but that also creates and sustains the very possibility of its existence (for example, through laws that not only protect the right to private property but also appropriately seek to restrain its use for the sake of the common good).

As a result, business corporations minimally should not interfere with the creation and sustenance of these countervailing institutions, even when short-term clashes of interest and power may dictate otherwise. This imperative is especially relevant in less developed countries, which typically have not yet generated such social infrastructure (cf. DeGeorge, 1993). In some cases, it may even mean substantial participation within those emergent institutions. In other cases, it may mean opposition to the views or interests of these institutions, for instance if bribery or corruption is present. Such institution can work in opposition to society's well-being if they function poorly or improperly, but the corporation should not oppose their right to function and develop.

Striving for Ecological Sustainability

Finally, business corporations must be more fully responsible for the impacts of their activities on the natural environment and seek to minimize environmental harm. Human progress, especially as evidenced through economic activity and technological change, can be viewed as the gradual recognition of and response to "the tragedy of the commons" (cf. Hardin, 1968). Historically, technology is both a part of the problem and a part of the solution. Recent human history, especially during the two hundred years, has seen a steady growth in human population, due largely to scientific discoveries and technological advances. These advances have enhanced our ability to sustain ever larger human populations within a fixed ecological environment. Agricultural technologies have allowed us to increase the carrying capacities of land to produce higher crop yields. Medical technologies and improvements in hygiene and sanitation have allowed us to lower infant mortality and decrease death rates: we keep more people alive longer. Engineering technologies have allowed us to obtain more useable energy from fossil fuels and more efficient and sophisticated uses of raw materials, making possible dramatic increases in economic standards of living across most of the globe. The aggregate result is ever-increasing demands and stress put upon the earth's natural resources and ecosystems to sustain ever larger numbers of humans at ever higher standards of living.

In a sense, technological advance has made us "victims of our own success." At some point within any "closed" ecological system, the demands made by organisms upon the nutrients in the environment reach and exceed its carrying capacity, resulting in ecological instability within the system. Clearly, technological progress brings our economic activities ever closer to the earth's carrying capacity, although precise measurement of that carrying capacity is elusive and not fully known. Hence, the general challenge for the human species on earth is to manage our activities and use our natural environment in ways that do not reach and exceed the earth's carrying capacity. This implies the need to bring human population growth under control. While the rate of population growth is declining in many parts of the world, we are still nowhere near the point of "zero population growth" (where births balance deaths and do not add to overall population numbers) globally. If we struggle with ecological limits with six billion people, what will our struggles look like at ten or fifteen billion, a possibility in the next century? Are we fast approaching the earth's overall limits? Indeed, some argue that the carrying capacities of some local ecosystems have already been exceeded, for instance in parts of Africa and Asia. Can these trends be reversed, or is the damage already irreversible? Admittedly, managing human reproductive patterns is not a primary concern for business—its primary responsibility lodges in other social institutions such as government and family. Nevertheless, this larger social concern with severe ecological impacts will affect business's capacity to engage its own practices in ecologically sustainable ways.

Technological innovations will also be a vital part of effective solutions to the potential tragedy of the commons, insofar as technology also seeks to develop ever more efficient means to generate energy from sources of fuel and useful products from raw materials. This can result in lower consumption of raw materials in production and of sources of fuel in the creation of usable energy.

In a competitive global market economy, the challenge will be to find market-friendly and fair ways to more effectively push the full array of social benefits and environmental costs into the market price of products and services. The aim is long-term sustainable development, which seeks to use the earth's resources to create economic well-being in ways that do not prevent future generations from doing the same. Put simply and crudely, we must not "use up" the earth's finite resources in ways that cannot be sustained over the long-term.

This imperative requires that business corporations, where possible, voluntarily find ways to make their operations more "environmentally friendly" through efforts that reduce use of raw materials and that minimize harmful pollution outputs. Where unilateral efforts may not be possible due to potential competitive disadvantage, it also requires that corporations advocate appropriate coordination and standardization of corporate practices. Examples include voluntary coordinated industry-wide efforts such as the "Responsible Care" program sponsored by the U.S. Chemical Manufacturers Association, which has demonstrated tremendous progress in reducing toxic chemical waste from manufacturing processes and in strengthening safety standards for companies and local communities. In most cases, it also includes governmental regulation aimed at long-term environmental sustainability and whose burdens and costs are applied fairly across industries to create a "level playing field."

In a global economy, the imperative of environmental sustainability will also require increased collaborative efforts between the private sector and governments of nation-states as they seek together to craft mutually agreeable standards of environmental protection. A prime example is the Montreal Protocol and subsequent agreements that will result in the global termination of the production and sale of the chlorofluorocarbon products reputed to contribute to the stratospheric destruction of the earth's vital ozone layer. This precedent-setting example of global collaboration involved support by industry leaders such as the DuPont Corporation as well as governments throughout the world and across the economic spectrum of "rich" and "poor" nations.

This imperative of environmental sustainability is grounded in the theological premise that God created the earth and all of its life forms. This divine creation imputes a sacred quality to the well-functioning of nature and its ecosystems. While the Genesis creation account declares that humans have a special place in nature and are mandated to make use of nature for human flourishing, it also asserts that this relationship with nature is one of stewardship and caretaking, not domination and manipulation. Hence, the "common good" toward which a Christian ethic aims must be expanded beyond the human community to include, in some fashion, the long-term sustainability of the larger community of life itself.

The Governance and Regulation of Business Corporations

Business corporations never exist in a social vacuum; rather they are always part of a larger social fabric, and it is better if it is in context of a flourishing civil society, as I have argued above. But even in these societies, the power they exercise is shaped by a myriad of internal and external factors and influences that need to be identified and subject to ethical analysis if the principles of productive justice are to be actualized. In countries like the United States, there is no totally "free market" or unfettered, unrestrained corporation free to pursue its interests without constraint in regard to its effects on other stakeholders and the larger society. Rather, our system is more aptly characterized as "regulated market" capitalism. This is less so, at least provisionally, in some newly emerging market economies in rapidly changing societies, such as Russia, as well as some less developed nations attempting to move out of poverty, although they have not yet developed sufficient infrastructure, either formal or informal, to restrain business behavior in appropriate ways. Indeed, some have characterized the current transitional political economic situation in Russia as "cowboy capitalism" or "mafia capitalism" for its higher levels of lawlessness. Under the regime of the former Soviet government, certain legal developments appropriate to productive justice were not only suspect, but outlawed—including adequate protection of private property, provision for interest rates and finance, equitable regulations for industry-wide activities, and rights to incorporate. The transition to a quasi-market economy without adequate legal channels for economic activity thus compounded the effects of rapid shifts in social mobility, as some became prosperous almost overnight and others saw their standards of living drop significantly due to the collapse of guaranteed employment, insufficient access to new capital, and the general weakening of a social safety net. Most observers consider this more chaotic, less regulated state of affairs to be temporary and far from optimal, because it is laden with practices of bribery, usury, corruption, protectionism, and personal influence peddling in the guise of bureaucratic regulation. Such behaviors are not only rejected by the international community but, one might predict, will also be found increasingly intolerable by citizens of Russian society as they aspire toward full social development and begin to draw distinctions between activities that had been labeled "capitalist" and evil. The situation stands as a rather striking illustration of the fact that "regulated capitalism" will more likely serve as the better social goal for newly emergent market economies, including those in less developed societies.

Since the question has never been whether or not to regulate, but only how much and in what way, my aim at this point is to consider more closely what mechanisms, both internal to its governance and external (in the form of both legal and governmental, as well as nonlegal social and cultural restraints) should shape and regulate a corporation's activities. Furthermore, I want to consider how the content of a transformative theological perspective and an ethic of productive justice might distinctively shape our normative expectations of governance and regulation. In other words, how should the business corporation rightly be governed and regulated to maximize its purpose—to generate wealth in ways that are profitable and serve the common good?

Questions of governance and regulation force us to clarify our understandings of "public" and "private," for their many definitions can make their uses confusing in social discourse. In some vocabularies, the very term "private sector" means to distinguish business organizations from "public sector," or governmental agencies. In this sense, "public" refers to formal institutions of government directly, whose authority resides (in the context of the United States) in the powers granted by the Constitution and is shaped by a public will expressed democratically through the citizenry (one person, one vote). In this sense, "private" also refers to organizations that pursue their ends (goods and services) for a profit to shareholders, as opposed to other nongovernmental organizations, sometimes referred to as independent, third sector, or nonprofit organizations, which conduct their affairs without shareholders and without the need to generate profits for such owners. Hence, in this way of using the term, business corporations are not "public" institutions in that they are not owned or managed directly by government. As we shall see, we reject such an arrangement on moral grounds for its harmful tendencies to place inordinate power in the hands of one social sector, the political one.

In other uses, however, business corporations are under "public scrutiny," and increasingly so, in the sense that their conduct is regulated not only formally by government, but informally and probably more significantly by influences from society's third or independent sector, as well as by the custodians of the religious and cultural values that constitute a society's undergirding "ethos." Religious groups and leaders make public statements and preach against various economic evils. The press investigates violations of the public trust and shapes public opinion. Scholars teach courses and write books that challenge behaviors and generate advocacy movements for or against various corporate policies in this country and around the world where this government has no jurisdiction. Unions and consumer groups publicly express their disagreements with, or approval of, business activities of this or that kind. This sort of activity takes place in a wider "public" than the earlier definition grasps. In this sense, it is inaccurate to say that business corporations, as "private" institutions, are beyond the scope of public accountability. Rather, they are accountable *both* to governmental jurisdiction *and* to larger social influences in a myriad of ways. The appropriate question, therefore, is devising the most effective kinds and mixes of accountability mechanisms and restraints so that business interests and larger social interests combine in ways that approximate a common good. Together, all these institutions combine to form the larger "public world" of civil society by which and in which our private selves become social selves, and the corporations live.

Corporate Governance

Internally, corporate governance involves the formal ways that businesses shape and enforce policies, set strategic directions, make decisions, and conduct their business practices. Such governance is shaped by factors that include the structure of corporation's ownership (e.g., publicly traded—those companies whose equity shares are traded openly in governmental-regulated stock exchanges; or privately held—those companies whose equity shares are not exchanged in such open markets); the composition and authority of its board of directors; its corporate by-laws and policies; and its unique history and corporate culture.

Publicly traded corporations, as well as other companies with boards of directors representing stockholders, are bound to legal requirements of fiduciary duty. As such, members of a board of directors, which formally governs the affairs of a corporation, have fiduciary duties to represent the financial interests of the shareholders. Generally, this duty is understood in terms of the financial health and well-being of the corporation, and in particular protecting the financial value of the equity owned by shareholders. In other words, boards of directors are required to oversee and evaluate management's actions to ensure that imprudent risks are not taken that would negatively affect the value of shareholder equity. In common parlance, the fiduciary duty associated with corporate governance generally is to pursue profitable investments for the sake of owners.

This fiduciary duty can be defended ethically, for it generally can be viewed as a partial embodiment of the Christian notion of stewardship and sustains important conditions for productive justice both in a market economy and in the business corporation. In most cases, the prudent management of risk on behalf of owners also generates benefits for other stakeholders as well as for the society at large. It is a rare corporation that consistently generates high rates of return for shareholders without also providing a product or service that benefits customers and is superior to the competition. Indeed, one fundamental learning from the collapse of centrally planned economies is that private capital generally is a more effective means to allocate financial risk for the provision of most of society's material needs than state-owned and state-directed systems of capital allocation and risk.

To be sure, private capital cannot fund all of the social goods and projects that require capital investment. Hence, various levels of government have been the primary providers of many services that require substantial capital investments, e.g., through public debt that supports education, physical infrastructure (such as roads), police and fire protection, general government services, and many utilities. Indeed, to make a theological-ethical defense of private capital is not to deny that our society's public investments might be solely underfunded, especially public education and the physical and social infrastructures of our cities. Hence, we can conclude by ethically affirming the principled fiduciary duty of boards of directors and senior managers to govern their organizations in ways that aim to prudently manage the financial risks borne by owners. For this system of capital risk management has proven more effective than the alternatives in allocating scarce capital to meet society's material aspirations.

But with respect to corporate governance, a transformative ethic that advocates the creation of wealth in ways that are profitable and advance the common good of society implies duties that include but also move beyond those to owners. Corporate wealth is not always generated in ways that are consistent with society's general well-being and are in the interests of most other stakeholders; sometimes it is generated in ways that are illegal, or in ways that, while legal, nevertheless still violate larger social interests in egregious ways. Laws are primarily reactive mechanisms of social control, usually enacted to prohibit a previously legal action that has caused social harm. In other words, this transformative position, unlike the standard, secular, minimalist view, argues that a corporation's duties do not end with owners (and with minimal adherence to laws). Hence, directors and senior managers must consider the corporation's impacts on a larger array of stakeholder interests as they engage in corporate governance. How such interests get factored into governance structures, strategic corporate planning, and general corporate decision making is open to debate and can be embodied within a variety of creative structural possibilities.

Some argue that corporate governance can most effectively demonstrate public accountability to society's "common good" through the promulgation and effective enforcement of governmental laws and regulations. In other words, moral agency resides primarily outside the corporation in the public sphere of government, and not within the walls of the corporate boardroom and senior executive office. While government regulation is an indispensable component to socially responsible business conduct, which will be discussed in more depth below, it is still a reactive mechanism, necessary but insufficient, to optimize a transformative ethical vision of the role of the business corporation in society. For external regulation still begs the question of whether and how a corporation can proactively account for its wider impacts on society as it pursues wealth for its owners. Debates quickly arise as to whether and how much a corporation's board of directors can attempt to take into account the interests of various stakeholders without coming into direct conflict with its legal fiduciary duties to owners. Such legal debates and tensions can be real, often complex, and beyond the scope of this essay to probe. Yet some states have gone so far as to pass laws permitting boards of directors to consider stakeholder interests in addition to shareholders.

The practical means by which corporations attempt to respond to larger social interests and integrate them into their decision making can vary widely from culture and legal environment. But some argue that larger social interests will not be adequately considered until the structure and membership of corporate boards change to reflect better those larger constituent groups. Hence, employee interests and local community interests, for instance, might be more effectively served by having such groups represented directly on boards of directors. While such a model has been practiced in some European nations through union representation on corporate boards, it is not widespread in the United States. Instead, the "voice" of employee interests in the United States has traditionally been "heard" through more adversarial mechanisms outside the corporate boardroom— via union negotiations, strikes, and threats of strikes. The challenge, thus, is to consider whether larger stakeholder interests such as employees can be factored more integrally into the representation and deliberation of corporate governance itself.

Yet the seeds of such a movement are present in some efforts to broaden and strengthen the participation of "outside directors" (those who do not hold management positions within the company itself). The primary value of outside directors is to better insure that a board has a necessary critical perspective sufficiently independent of internal management as it evaluates management's performance on behalf of shareholder interests. Without ignoring a board's inherent fiduciary duties vigilantly to represent shareholder interests, are there not creative possibilities for expanding the diversity of interests and backgrounds represented on a board in order to enhance sensitivities and predispositions to wider stakeholder interests as well? For instance, the German provisions for *Mitbestimmung*, or "codetermination" between labor and management, demanded by the Allies after World War II, brought representatives of the workers into the boardroom and reduced the polarizations of the two. And in this country, might we not see more sustained and measurable progress in creating and sustaining diverse workforces if boards of directors themselves had more female and/or minority representation? Yet the representation of women and persons of color on the boards of directors of large publicly-traded corporations has shown little change for decades. Women still constitute less that 10 percent and persons of color well under 5 percent of the membership of corporate boards—percentages far below their larger levels of employment within their organizations.

Enhanced attention to "common good" kinds of issues as illustrated by the proposed ethical criteria in the previous section can also become integrated into corporate governance through the efforts of growing shareholder activist movements. For more than twenty-five years, groups of institutional investors have participated in coordinated efforts to file shareholder resolutions with corporations in which they own stock. This filing process, protected through regulations by the Securities and Exchange Commission (SEC), produces resolutions that request or demand various actions by a corporation that address an array of social and ethical responsibility issues (e.g., labor relations, environmental concerns, community relations, or harmful products).[4] When satisfying various procedural criteria established by the SEC, these resolutions sometimes come to a vote by corporate shareholders, although rarely do more than a few percent of shareholders support any one resolution. More typically, though, this filing process results in informal negotiations between the filers and management and the eventual withdrawal of the formal resolution if satisfactory outcomes are negotiated between the shareholders and representatives of management. While the value and role of this movement is subject to debate among its proponents and skeptics, its impact seems to be in its capacity, through the democratic mechanisms protected by shareholder rights, to persuade and even to pressure corporate boards and managements to address a larger array of ethical and social issues important to various groups in society. Protestant denominations, Roman Catholic religious orders, and institutional pension funds have been at the forefront of this shareholder movement.[5]

Individual investors also have the capacity to influence corporate governance and the impacts of corporations on the larger society through selective investments in "socially screened" investment funds. Some such funds are independent mutual funds open to the general public. Indeed, the first socially screened mutual fund in the United States, the Pax World Fund, was established in 1970 through the leadership of United Methodist clergypersons, among others. Others are available through many large employer pension funds. In the latter, member participants of defined contribution pension plans are typically provided an array of investment fund alternatives, among which are some investment funds that include ethical investment criteria, in addition to traditional financial criteria (e.g., type of investment instrument such as stocks or bonds, and levels of risk and return). Among those organizational pension funds at the forefront of this growing movement have been religious denominations, universities and other educational institutions, as well as other large nonprofits and municipal and state governments.

Such ethical "screens" are typically two types, negative and positive. Negative criteria screen out investments in companies whose products or practices are deemed inconsistent with the espoused social values of the fund. Typical negative criteria can include: no weapons of mass destruction (although companies producing other types of weapons and defense products are typically not excluded unless the investment criteria espouse strict pacifism), no tobacco products, no hard alcoholic beverages (companies producing beer and wine are typically not screened out), avoidance of some employment practices deemed especially unethical (e.g., companies with demonstrated track records in discrimination, egregiously harmful environmental practices, child and prison labor in foreign countries). Positive screens seek investments in companies whose products or practices are deemed to have exemplary social value or importance such as re-investment and employment in poor communities. These positive screens typically encourage selective investments when all other relevant financial criteria are also satisfied. As the monetary value of capital investments under various types of "social screens" continues to grow, this conventional democratic mechanism within the system of capital ownership will become even more powerful as a means for gradualist corporate transformation. It serves as a strategic means for owners of capital to express their moral convictions about how business corporations ought to conduct themselves in ways that are consistent with larger moral visions of the good society. Within other societies, with other religious and cultural values, one can imagine ways in which owners of capital also can attempt to make their stewardship of property consistent with deeper religious convictions. Islamic tradition, for instance, prohibits charging interest on loans (a prohibition that will likely become more and more unsustainable as fundamentalist Islam confronts modernity—in this case global structures of financial capital markets).

Finally, corporate governance can be transformed to account

more fully for the larger array of considerations embedded within the common good by creating and sustaining internal accountability mechanisms to measure and improve a corporation's ethical performance in various areas. Those areas can include nondiscrimination and workplace diversity, local community relationships, and environmental protection. These concerns, and many more, are also treated within a complex host of government laws and regulatory requirements that bear upon and restrain the scope of a corporation's activities. At the same time, though, they can also be areas that corporations choose to prioritize and pursue above and beyond the scope of the external regulatory environment. Just as many corporations have attempted to transform their philosophies, structures, and practices around heightened commitments to quality, so can they make similar efforts on other ethical fronts. For instance, many manufacturers have instituted radical commitments to environmental protection and sustainability that have moved far beyond adherence to minimal regulatory requirements concerning pollution emissions to embrace all the ways in which a corporation's products, use of raw materials, and production processes might be modified to reduce or even eliminate any harmful environmental consequences. Some have even aimed to become "zero emission" companies, akin to quality efforts to achieve "zero quality defects" in production.

Corporations make such efforts not only because they may be beneficial to the larger society and natural environment but because they will also usually generate short-term and/or long-term financial benefits to the organization as well by reducing production costs or avoiding more costly government regulatory solutions. Such efforts are more likely to be successful when they include the following components: clearly defined and measurable goals and objectives; designated persons with clear authority and oversight of such initiatives (usually senior officers reportable directly to the chief executive officer and/or the board of directors); discrete and measurable action plans and timetables for implementation; formal mechanisms for regular evaluation and revisions of the goals and performance; and direct reporting mechanisms to the board of directors so that such areas become serious and measurable concerns embedded within the structures and patterns of corporate governance. Admittedly, such attention to multiple social concerns and objectives makes corporate governance and management more complex. Such objectives cannot always be easily coordinated. Scarce resources may not make all attainable within given time frames, especially when efficiency and short-term profitability constraints bear down, sometimes relentlessly, upon a corporation. Yet such complexity will be a fundamental condition of corporate governance in a global market economy.

External Regulation

Corporations function within a web of external economic constraints (e.g., market and industry trends) and countervailing social forces and centers of institutional power, all of which can affect corporate behavior. Within most industrialized democracies, the wider fabric of background institutions that constitute the civil society works to enable, shape, and restrain corporate power. Indeed, law itself both grants corporations the very right to exist and to protect their affairs from unlawful interference by others, and it provides for the rights to sue corporations, to strike against them, and to boycott them. Law and regulation also strive to "smooth out the rough edges of capitalism" and prevent or correct some harmful social effects of business activity. An effective balance of these countervailing institutional powers is desirable for the well-functioning society and for appropriate social control of business activity. Seeking the right balance is an ever-moving target in a constantly changing world. But such a balance is a critical component of a good society, for it helps to provide the institutional and structural conditions that prevent any single sector from exercising inordinate power to the detriment of the common good.

Creating and maintaining such an institutional balance of power in the global economy of the twenty-first century and beyond will present new challenges, not only for industrialized nations but especially for less developed countries. All nations, regardless of level of economic development or type of government, will face the common challenges of economic globalization and revisionist thinking about the changing roles of government in society. For industrialized democracies under continued fiscal pressures from electorates, the challenge will be to adapt the regulatory functions of government in ways that are cost effective and flexible to changing global economic realities. For newly emergent industrialized market democracies in transition from totalitarian societies with centrally planned economies, the challenge is more daunting and radical—not only to deconstruct economic monopolies that were owned and controlled by governments along with the entire legal infrastructure that sustained them, but also to create competitive market-based private sector institutions where they were previously largely nonexistent along with an entirely new set of laws and government regulatory functions much more limited in scope than those that preceded them. Concurrent is the deeper challenge for religion and other cultural value institutions to promulgate a new fabric of moral values and virtues that support a radically changed political economy. This seems nothing less than the creation of an entirely new social infrastructure and moral value system *ex nihilo*. It is no surprise, therefore, that the regulatory track record of governments vis-à-vis newly emergent private sectors in countries such as Russia is mixed and uneven at best. Corruption, slow legislative processes, as well as grossly uneven regulatory enforcement should not be unexpected in such a difficult transition period.

For less developed countries, the challenge is not only to downsize much of the direct government involvement in public sector economic activity, to eliminate protectionist trade policies and practices, and to strengthen the concomitant macroeconomic nurturing of vibrant competitive private sectors, but also, perhaps ironically, to strengthen the capacity of law and governmental power effectively to create and enforce appropriate regulation of their newly emerging and growing private sectors. For instance, adequate protection of property rights, worker and consumer protection, as well as adequate creation and enforcement of environmental protection, typically emerge only as bribery, corruption, and other nondemocratic political influences lose their distorting grip on the application of social rules and as societies generate sufficient levels of widespread economic prosperity to afford the added social cost of an appropriate regulatory infrastructure. The goal is not the absence of government, but rather its restructuring and redirection, and in some vital areas its growth and strengthening (especially in the regulatory arena).

With the decline of statism, nation-state and lower level governments will lose *some* capacity to manage and control social outcomes generally and, as a consequence, business behavior in particular. For instance, as industrialized democracies continue to downsize government due to fiscal pressures as well as changing political preferences of electorates, their capacity to enforce government regulations may become more strained. Such downsizing will force governments to generate more efficient and innovative ways to create the positive outcomes that regulation seeks. For instance, efforts to reduce bureaucratic "red tape" associated with regulatory compliance will likely continue as we attempt to assess and measure the fuller "costs" associated with various forms of compliance. Indeed, electorates in countries such as the United States are becoming more intent on making "cost-benefit" evaluations of regulations in order to assess their value and effectiveness to society.

Some older "command and control" forms of regulation that sought to control corporate behavior based strictly upon disincentives, such as financial penalties for noncompliance, may need to give way to a broader array of strategies, which include positive as well as negative incentives. This is already taking place in some areas of environmental protection; in some industries, corporations that exceed certain air quality regulations not only avoid financial penalties but also can benefit financially from such exemplary performance by selling pollution permits to others who provisionally do not. Suddenly, regulatory strategy becomes two-pronged, not only seeking to dissuade harmful social actions but also seeking to provide measurable market-friendly incentives that support corporate practices with benign social impacts. This type of two-pronged regulatory strategy, driven in part by growing governmental fiscal constraints, also suggests the value of collaboration and cooperation between government and private sector firms and industry groups whose mutual aim is the creation of adequate and cost-effective controls on business behavior, be they voluntary and internally generated or mandatory and externally driven.

Power will continue to disperse from government to business and to other nongovernmental social groups, making institutional decision making and social policy formation more complex and collaborative. This more diffuse pattern of social power will also continue to shape the ways that corporations exercise self-governance and decision making as they negotiate with more stakeholders than in the past (cf. Kuhn and Shriver, 1991). For instance, as the web of special interest groups representing various stakeholder interests continues to deepen and broaden in democratic societies, and as these groups continue to become more adept in their capacities to communicate their messages through the media to the general public, corporations will be less able to ignore or deflect their concerns. Many corporations will be increasingly amenable to crafting mutually agreeable solutions to these stakeholder concerns not only to avoid potentially harmful consequences to their businesses (e.g., negative public relations campaigns, or the threat of increased governmental regulation) but also to generate long-term good will and trust around social issues that can help to create the very conditions for sustained, long-term corporate growth and profitability. We have seen this process, for instance, in informal negotiations between professional sports associations and groups seeking greater involvement by minorities in the ownership and management of professional sports organizations.

On the environmental front, we have seen corporations and environmental groups move from adversarial relationships of public confrontation to mutual collaboration and partnership. In the early 1990s, for instance, the Environmental Defense Fund joined its agenda and expertise with the McDonald's Corporation to identify ways in which McDonald's could reduce its packaging and use of paper products and thus its contributions to the solid waste stream. This collaboration resulted in ground-breaking changes in the packaging of its products, which were not only well-received by customers but also led most other competitors in the industry to follow McDonald's, the industry leader. These changes were beneficial to the environment, enhanced McDonald's reputation as a more environmentally responsible company, reduced production costs by decreasing the use of packaging, did not result in any loss of market share, and provided the impetus for an industry-wide sea change in the more responsible use of packaging. While we might still challenge on larger moral grounds the social benefits and costs of a culture so dependent upon "fast food," we can nevertheless count the above as an example of multiple-stakeholder collaboration resulting in a "win-win" solution benefiting all relevant parties. This type of corporate collaboration is an example of the restraining and shaping power that social interests and institutions external to the corporation can have on the internal governance and behavior of a firm.

With the ascendancy of an integrated global economy, economic activities will extend across political borders that become more and more permeable. Questions of adequate and appropriate regulation of business corporations, especially by government, show their face anew in more pronounced and profound ways. For more than a century, as multinational corporations have slowly expanded their role and scope across the globe, we have raised the now classic question of whether and how nation-state governments can function as an effective countervailing power to regulate global business. This question became more pronounced in the 1960s and 1970s as those remaining less developed countries under colonial rule made their final transitions to post-colonial existence, and as poverty and political instability continued to persist in large portions of the Third World at a time when multinational corporations generally were expanding their reach and involvement in many of those countries.

Much analysis at the time alarmingly argued that such growing international corporate power would result in serious deleterious effects, unless strongly controlled (centrist and moderate leftist positions), if not eliminated (radical leftists). Barnet and Müller's *Global Reach: The Power of the Multinational Corporations* (1974) and others in similar ways have argued that multinational corporate interests diverged substantially from larger public interests, not only in the Third World, but even the First World. They would continue to cause harm if unchecked by appropriate countervailing political power, they argued. Yet the danger was not only that growing international corporate power would allow multinational corporations more and more to avoid the regulatory jurisdiction of single nation-state governments. It was more profoundly that such power might change the very nature of the nation-state so as to render it permanently incapable of preventing global corporations from pursuing their relentless, hegemonic reach of aggrandizement as they brought the entire world under their integrated, rational control with ultimate accountability to no one but themselves—the epitome not of political, but of economic tyranny. Both liberation theologians and Marxist theorists of political economy, such as Wallerstein (1976/1980, 1983), offered interpretations of capitalism as a world system of domination and exploitation. They shared some of the same analysis and advocated more radical solutions to harmful corporate domination—generally its elimination. Indeed, while Wallerstein is notable for his breadth and comprehensiveness of analysis, he is merely illustrative of the kinds of radical critiques that became mainstreamed into intellectual thought. If corporate power is inherently exploitive, its political regulation is not an adequate social solution. Rather, a qualitatively different structure of social power and economic organization is one brought directly under the control and management of government, with its assumption of benign democratic control by bureaucrats or "the people." While the terms of the debate have shifted somewhat in the post-socialist world, causing more radical solutions to corporate power to drop out of the equation, the question of adequate regulation and control of business corporations, increasingly global in scope, nevertheless remains.

Clearly, our basic and legitimate fear of corporate power in an integrated global economy is that it might have an overall exploitive or harmful impact on society that is inconsistent with the general public interest and society's and nature's long-term common good. The following long-term scenario might provide the kinds of evidence that could substantiate those fears. A continued global shift of production to manufacturing sites in less developed countries with lower costs of production could result in decreased levels of prosperity *globally* over the long term. This same shift involves a trend from unionized to nonunionized workers, resulting in a deterioration of the condition and rights of workers globally (e.g., in worker health and safety, rights to free speech and to organize, increased levels of discrimination) over the long-term. This production shift from countries with highly developed environmental protection laws and enforcement to lowly developed ones results in an overall decline in environmental standards and quality in the long term as well. And more generally, the fear that this increased economic activity in less developed countries fails to result in marked and measurable improvements in the development of the myriad of just background institutions that citizens of democratic countries such as the United States take for granted as necessary conditions for the good society, as already discussed.

In other words, many fear that the increased mobility of corporate power and production in an integrated global economy will result in the steady *global decline* of living standards and especially of the qualitative social measures of the good society that we have attributed so significantly to the role of government regulation and of healthy and well-developed independent sector institutions in industrialized democratic societies. The fear of some is that the relatively workable balance of countervailing powers in industrialized democracies that has created not only economic prosperity but also the myriad other social benefits of the good civil society will be harmfully and irrevocably upset. Instead of a "rising tide" of economic prosperity *and* qualitative social expectations, we will see a slow and steady sinking of prosperity and quality of life toward a "lowest common denominator" that makes most of the world worse off (except perhaps those powerful owners and managers of large business corporations who are controlling the process).

This worst-case scenario could be an eventual outcome of a shift of power toward private sector institutions in an integrated global economy increasingly impervious to external restraints, especially by nation-state governments. Such a result—entailing the demise of sustainable, global democratic civil society—clearly would not be consistent with the moral imperatives of a tranformative ethic whose vision of corporate purpose is to generate wealth in ways that are profitable and that serve the common good by contributing to the development of an ecologically sustainable global civil society. Thus, sustaining existing effective regulatory mechanisms and creating new ones appropriate to the challenges of the new economic context will be vital components to this larger moral vision.

Many factors mitigate against the above worst-case scenario. One such factor is the end of the cold war and the corresponding demise of the bipolar world; this has not only diminished the social costs of military defense, which can impede real economic and social development, but has also dramatically enhanced the prospects for genuine consensus about the roles and moral expectations of society's basic institutions, including business corporations and the appropriate regulatory functions of government. Another such factor, one that seems to be a distinctive trend in the new globalized economic context, is that problems and issues that once were considered to be purely local or unique to some regions but not others (e.g., air pollution, toxic wastes, unsanitary water supplies, overpopulation, high uses of energy, worker rights, consumer protection) will increasingly be seen as global in scope or impact. The actions of each player will increasingly affect the others, creating more situations of mutual interdependence and more frequently requiring negotiated solutions characterized by mutual cooperation and accountabilities.

Common problems and issues will continue to move across nation-states, requiring multilateral and multisector collaboration and agreements. Prominent issues will include environmental degradation, energy and natural resource conservation, fair trade and protection of property rights, and the rights of workers. These challenges will increasingly require collaborative and strategically coordinated solutions negotiated less by unilateral assertions of power and authority and more by negotiation, often complex and sometimes conflictual, among a multilateral host of players, including multilateral organizations, governments, corporations, and nongovernmental organizations. Notable examples include fair trade (e.g., the most recent General Agreement on Tariffs and Trade [GATT] treaty, which led to the formation of the World Trade Organization to monitor its compliance); the rights of workers (e.g., the European Union's standardization of social policy and labor laws); and the many issues of environmental degradation and protection. The most prominent example of collaborative success may be the Montreal Protocol and subsequent agreements phasing out the use of chlorofluorocarbon products harmful to the stratospheric ozone layer. In sum, our emergent model is likely to be a new kind of collaborative matrix, perhaps federalist in nature, of institutions providing various forms and levels of international constraints.

As mentioned earlier, it is this last area of environmental sustainability that will likely present the most daunting regulatory challenges and will require the most sustained and comprehensive efforts at creating international environmental agreements and treaties. Those challenges will concern biodiversity (especially the threats of increased species extinction rates due to continued high rates of tropical deforestation), global warming (possible threats of global temperature increases due especially to increased human use of carbon-generating fossil fuels), fresh water supplies, and continued high population growth rates.

The challenge of creating this matrix of adequate regulatory mechanisms to manage these actual and potential problems cuts to the heart of the definition and limits of national sovereignty. For most forms of multilateral collaboration and agreement require that each national actor accept limits on its own freedom of action. This will increasingly involve matters over which nation-state governments traditionally have understood themselves to have absolute sovereignty, such as currency, social policy, and use of natural resources. Within the multination federalist model of the European Union, for instance, nation-state governments have agreed to cede some sovereign authority to a new and slowly evolving supranational regional level of government. Much authority vested in this new layer of government to establish more standardized laws and policies has direct impacts on business corporations in the region as they must adhere to new sets of regulations on their activities. One important question, therefore, will be the extent to which the evolving regional federalist regulatory system of the European Union can serve as a model for other regions of the world or for other types of problems, notably environmental, involving business corporations and impacting stakeholders around the globe. Because the value and likelihood that we can create a "world government" level of political power with substantial implications for the scope of nation-state sovereignty seems remote, we will more likely depend upon more modest regional configurations or matrices of political and social authority and upon problem-specific multilateral treaties and covenants, as well as constantly evolving nation-state laws and regulatory systems, to attempt the effective creation of appropriate levels of countervailing political and social power in the regulation of global business.

Finally, with a shift toward more production in lower-cost, less developed countries, global corporations will more frequently find themselves in situations in which their own exercise of power takes place within different configurations of countervailing power. Most notably, many of the less developed countries have not yet created a system of background institutions strong enough to provide the systems of protection for private sector activity and property, as well as of safeguards against abuses of private sector power, that are usually in place in industrialized democracies; nor have they developed a private sector strong enough to act as a countervailing power to a socially dominating and often corrupt government. The moral challenge for corporations in such situations, where there is no adequate countervailing power, becomes the exercise of voluntary restraint from the use of corporate power in ways that can knowingly cause egregious harm to other stakeholders and to the larger common good of that society. This voluntary restraint is aided by the presence of a strong internal corporate culture with clearly defined, promulgated, and enforced ethical standards universally applicable wherever a corporation does business. This moral challenge also implies that corporations should actively support, in ways that are prudent and feasible, the creation and nurture of appropriate countervailing institutions when they are absent or not yet fully developed.

Conclusion

In sum, the ethic I am advocating here draws upon fundamental Christian theological notions of conversion and the common good to argue constructively for a theory of "productive justice" that can guide the business corporations as they assume a greater role in a global market economy. The special social purpose of the corporation is to generate wealth profitably and in ecologically sustainable ways that serve humanity's common good and observe Godly principles in a dynamic, rapidly changing, globalizing era. The new situation invites this discussion, clarification, and honoring of "productive justice," by adding it to our more traditional ethical vocabulary that has focused predominantly on "distributive justice" and "commutative justice."

I have attempted to make this case not only upon principled and theoretical grounds but also by an analysis of empirical conditions, driven by an appreciation of both historical developments and future prospects. Those who are not persuaded could attempt to refute these lines of thinking on principled and theoretical grounds, arguing that I have not adequately utilized fundamental Christian theological notions to show sufficient coherence between contemporary capitalist business practice and the basic norms of Christian faith. Or they could argue pragmatically and empirically that the configurations of social institutions here advocated will not perform well in practice or that some other configuration of institutions (e.g., socialist or subsistence economics) would function more effectively to serve human well-being in just and ecologically sustainble ways. Yet if we have learned anything from the errors and short-comings of much of twentieth-century Christian economic ethics, it is that these two methods of argument cannot be pulled very far apart from one another before one runs the risk of drawing impractical judgments and conclusions about economic life and the other becomes unprincipled and ungrounded. Many of this century's most sophisticated and "well-crafted" theoretical arguments within Christian theology and ethics proposed socialist economic arrangements that were at best weak and at worst severely flawed in their descriptive and pragmatic dimensions. Hence, with respect to economic life, good theology must include (but dare not be exhausted by) a pragmatic test. Good theory must, in some real way, work; and what works must be tested for its qualitative impacts on persons and society.

In this connection, we must embrace the fact that capitalism's major systemic alternative, centrally planned socialism, has recently faded from the global scene, leaving market-based economic arrangements, nearly universally, to provide the contours for economic development. I interpret this trend not as a manifestation of pervasive sin but more as a possible indicator of divine providence in the world. In this sense the theologically grounded ethic of productive justice resembles, in certain ways, the classical natural law theory embodied within key streams of Roman Catholic ethics, Reinhold Niebuhr's Christian Realism, and H. Richard Niebuhr's "incarnational/synthetist" type of transformative ethics. This nearly global coalescing around a common set of economic institutions, practices, and values can be interpreted as a type of theological natural order, imperfect and flawed because tainted by sin, yet affirmed in practice for its capacity, better than the institutional alternatives, to contribute to human welfare at this point in human history. This argument is not unlike those within the political realm with respect to democratic institutions and practices.

With respect to individuals and personal fulfillment, it affirms also the moral value of effective participation within economic life, and thus within business corporations, seen in the context of a vibrant civil society. Good productive practice, nurtured by the conditions of productive justice, can embody a dimension of the Christian's vocation in the world and thus be affirmed as providential.

This ethical affirmation is not an uncritical "baptism" or sacralizing of capitalist institutions, for its defense is not unconditional but conditional upon its performance—its capacity to satisfy at least minimal moral criteria of human, social, and ecological well-being. Indeed, it moves well beyond the "accommodative" and even "incarnational" types by underscoring Protestantism's conviction of the fundamental pervasiveness of sin built into the structure of temporal reality. Hence the necessity of accenting the "transformative" understanding capitalism and business corporations. They, like all aspects of political, familial, educational, and cultural existence, remain flawed and marred by sin yet open to the possibility of renewal and creative transformation under the sovereignty of God. This transformative possibility provides the opportunity or opening for Christians in society and within business corporations to "make a difference." Its practical embodiment implies, indeed requires, that such moral transformation to some extent be quantitative and measurable. Moral knowledge of the good cannot be so diffuse or illusive that we cannot formulate some at least minimal agreement about its constitutive features to be embodied within social practice. Moral agency within economic life and business corporations can result in moral progress. Yet the reality of sin forces the recognition that moral progress is never automatic and is under constant threat of regression and decay. Twentieth-century history is sufficient reminder of the episodic character of human existence, with extreme cycles of both horrific terror and also dramatic, exciting discovery and social progress. This transformative possibility also provides a vital and constructive role for religion in the modern world, as it seeks creatively to inform, shape, motivate, and inspire persons who participate within economic life, not only through work within business corporations but also through those in positions to influence the very structure of those institutions and practices.

Finally, this argument is empirically driven insofar as it depends upon the future prospects and performance of business corporations with a global market economy. Business corporations, and the system of market-based political and economic institutions and practices that sustain them, will be morally defensible not only on principled and theoretical grounds but also on their actual historical performance and practice. We live in a time that is arguably a new historical period, perhaps one of the most significant and profound for humanity and the earth. Corporations and markets, in combination with the appropriate supporting and countervailing political and independent sector institutions of civil society, either will or will not create the kinds of outcomes that humanity deems consistent with its deepest moral aspirations and expectations. Within a Christian ethical framework, those moral aspirations must include a fundamental commitment to alleviate poverty and also to respect environmental sustainability and ecological well-being. Within the emergent integrated global market economy, the fundamental commitment to alleviate poverty must be global in scope. Hence, if business corporations are to be the primary institutional mechanisms for the generation of wealth, their performance, over time, must contribute to the widespread alleviation of poverty throughout most portions of the globe.

This is not to argue that all regions of the world can, or should, reach economic standards of living comparable to those of the world's richest countries; indeed, this is not likely to be environmentally sustainable over the long term. But it is to demand that, over time, most regions of the world attain at least basic levels of material well-being consistent with the requirements of human fulfillment. Likewise, it is to demand that market-based economic arrangements continue to transform their practices in ways that move from environmentally unsustainable to environmentally sustainable patterns over the long term. This larger mandate is necessary not only for long-term human well-being but also for the survival and well-being of the larger community of life itself.

References

Atherton, John. *Christianity and the Market: Christian Social Thought for Our Times.* London: SPCK, 1992.

Benne, Robert. *The Ethic of Democratic Capitalism: A Moral Reassessment.* Philadelphia: Fortress Press, 1981.

Berger, Peter L. *The Capitalist Revolution: Fifty Propositions About Prosperity, Equality, and Liberty.* New York: Basic Books, 1986.

Cairncross, Frances. *Costing the Earth: The Challenge for Governments, the Opportunities for Business.* Boston: Harvard Business School Press, 1992.

Chewning, Richard C., John W. Eby, and Shirley J. Roels. *Business Through the Eyes of Faith.* San Francisco: Harper & Row, 1990.

Daly, Herman E. and John B. Cobb, Jr. *For the Common Good: Redirecting the Economy Toward Community, the Environment, and a Sustainable Future.* Boston: Beacon Press, 1989.

DeGeorge, Richard. *Competing with Integrity in International Business,* Oxford: Oxford University Press, 1993.

Friedman, Milton. *Capitalism and Freedom.* Chicago: University of Chicago Press, 1962.

————, and Rose Friedman. *Free to Choose: A Personal Statement.* New York: Harcourt, Brace, Jovanovich, 1979.

Fukuyama, Francis. *Trust: The Social Virtues and the Creation of Prosperity.* New York: Free Press, 1995.

Hardin, Garrett. "The Tragedy of the Commons." *Science,* Vol. 162, pp. 1243–48, 13 December 1968.

Hayek, Friedrich A. *Law Legislation and Liberty* (3 volumes). Chicago: University of Chicago Press, 1973, 1976, 1979.

John Paul II. *Centesimus Annus (On the Hundredth Anniversary of* Rerum Novarum). Papal Encyclical, 1991.

Krueger, David A. *Keeping Faith at Work: The Christian in the Workplace.* Nashville: Abingdon Press, 1994.

Kuhn, James W. and Donald W. Shriver, Jr. *Beyond Success: Corporations and Their Critics in the 1990s.* New York: Oxford University Press, 1991.

Maritain, Jacques. *Integral Humanism: Temporal and Spiritual Problems of a New Christendom.* Notre Dame: University of Notre Dame Press, 1973 (first published 1936).

————. *The Person and the Common Good.* Notre Dame: University of Notre Dame Press, 1966 (first published 1946).

Meeks, M. Douglas. *God the Economist: The Doctrine of God and Political Economy.* Minneapolis: Fortress Press, 1989.

Niebuhr, H. Richard. *Christ and Culture.* New York: Harper & Row, 1975 (first published in 1951).

————. *The Meaning of Revelation.* New York: Macmillan, 1960 (first published 1941).

Niebuhr, Reinhold. *The Nature and Destiny of Man*. 2 vols. New York: Charles Scribner's Sons, 1964 (first published 1941, 1943).

Novak, Michael. *Freedom With Justice: Catholic Social Thought and Liberal Institutions*. San Francisco: Harper & Row, 1984.

———. *The Spirit of Democratic Capitalism*. New York: Simon & Schuster, 1982.

———. *The Catholic Ethic and the Spirit of Capitalism*. New York: Free Press, 1993.

Preston, Ronald H. *Confusions in Christian Social Ethics: Problems for Geneva and Rome*. Grand Rapids: Wm. B. Eerdmans, 1994.

———. *Religion and the Ambiguities of Capitalism*. Cleveland: Pilgrim Press, 1993 (originally published by SCM Press in 1991).

———. *Religion and the Persistence of Capitalism*. London: SCM Press, 1979.

Rauschenbusch, Walter. *Christianity and the Social Crisis*. New York: Macmillan, 1907.

———. *A Theology of the Social Gospel*. New York: Macmillan, 1917.

Rawls, John. *A Theory of Justice*. Cambridge: Harvard University Press, 1971.

Ryan, John A. *A Better Economic Order*. New York: Harper, 1935.

———. *Distributive Justice: The Right and Wrong of Our Present Distribution of Wealth*. Third edition. New York: Macmillan, 1942.

———. *A Living Wage: Its Ethical and Economic Aspects*. New York: Macmillan, 1906.

Schumpeter, Joseph A. *History of Economic Analysis*. New York: Oxford University Press, 1954.

Stackhouse, Max L. *Public Theology and Political Economy: Christian Stewardship in Modern Society*. Grand Rapids: Wm. B. Eerdmans, 1987.

———, Peter L. Berger, Dennis P. McCann, and M. Douglas Meeks. *Christian Social Ethics in a Global Era*. Nashville, Abingdon Press, 1995.

———, Dennis P. McCann, and Shirley J. Roels (editors). *On Moral Business: Classical and Contemporary Resources for Ethics in Economic Life*. Grand Rapids: Wm B. Eerdmans, 1995.

Tillich, Paul. *The Socialist Decision*. New York: Harper & Row, 1977 (first published 1933).

Wallerstein, Immanuel. *Historical Capitalism*. London: Verso, 1983.

———. *The Modern World-System*, Vol. 1: *Capitalist Agriculture and the Origin of the European World-Economy in the Sixteenth Century* (1976), and Vol. 2: *Mercantilism and the Consolidation of the European World-Economy* (1980), New York: Academic Press.

World Commission on Environment and Development, *Our Common Future*. Oxford: Oxford University Press, 1987.

Chapter 2

Two Cheers and Two Reservations

Donald W. Shriver, Jr.

The Roman Catholic philosopher Jacques Maritain once remarked that students of ethics, intellectually speaking, are unhappy people. "Give us some guidelines for how we ought to behave," their audiences exclaim. So the ethicist voices some general principles, to which audiences reply, "Could you be more specific?" So the ethicist offers a few concrete illustrations of what it would mean to behave according to those principles. Then the audience demurs: "But that is so impractical."

As one possible case of ethical impracticality, in the history of one American business corporation, consider the following example. In the mid-1980s the government of South Africa offered a major American manufacturer of heavy equipment a contract worth some fifty million dollars. After a day of deliberating on the question of what business, if any, an American firm should undertake with a government devoted to the racist principle of apartheid, top management decided not to accept the contract, which was speedily picked up by a competing firm in Germany. Asked later why they turned down such a lucrative contract, the CEO replied, "It would have contradicted the character of our company."

As every participant in the South Africa sanctions debate of the 1980s will remember, argument over such a decision forced the arguers back to some basic contentions about the relations of economics, politics, and ethics. Some argued that there was little or no connection, conveniently segregating business decision from questions of the right or wrong of racial discrimination in a politically enforced ideology. Others, agreeing about the moral wrong of apartheid, urged pragmatic "constructive engagement," i.e. foreign companies in South Africa should use their economic leverage to defy certain aspects of apartheid (e.g. by training black workers) and thereby serving the same goal as the sanction-supporters.

Another party to the debate opposed sanctions as a measure sure to harm most the under- or unemployed masses of South African blacks. In reply to this moral concern, some leaders of South Africa churches stated that the moral-political evils of apartheid took precedence over temporary economic pain: "We are willing to suffer further poverty if that is the cost to us of putting pressure upon this evil system," they said.

In retrospect, it is now apparent that international sanctions did speed the collapse of apartheid in South Africa, but only in conjunction with the collapse of an external threat (the former Soviet Union) and the looming internal threat of mounting political violence. Predicting the future impact of any action by any persons or groups in a society is always risky, and that is one reason why sheer utilitarianism—justifying an action by its predictable results—seems always to *lack* a certain utility! Sometimes "doing the right thing for its own sake" is the only maxim worth falling back on. The American company was doing so when its leaders decided that the integrity of its "character" required them to defy the priority of profit and to observe an overriding hope for the coming of justice in a foreign land. That hope was a compound of economic, political, and moral thinking.

In response to David Krueger's challenging essay, it is pertinent to ask how four of his five principles of productive justice, in their relation to the common social good, got implemented, neglected, and ordered in this very case—efficiency, social benefit, justice to stakeholders, countervailing power. Concern for justice and human rights for the South African "stakeholders" was plainly uppermost in the decision while efficiency and profit for the company were reluctantly downgraded. In this case an American company acted as a "countervailing institution" within the business system itself. One could say that competition at its moral best sometimes pushes competitors to act more ethically than a monopoly is likely to act. Inside South Africa, the ecumenical churches, led by Desmond Tutu, were offering almost the only countervailing voice against the government. Especially crucial, in the managerial debate, must have been the assessment of the probable uses of the product in that South African society. The product happened to be motors for transportation systems, both civilian and military—a mixture of benefit to both some ordinary South Africans and those who enforced apartheid with "legitimate" violence. This latter strongly influenced this managerial debate: maybe machines for commerce were all right, but the military enforcement behind apartheid was something else, and the American company would have no control over the distribution of uses of its machines. Here surfaced the age-old ethical issue: benefit *for whom?*

Those of us who participated in the sanctions controversy during this era remember our perplexity over this very issue. As it happened, the CEO in this case was an active member of a Protestant denomination and a former lay president of the National Council of Churches. When he said that supplying transportation facilities for the South African government conflicted with the character of his company, he doubtless was reflecting his own character, which over many years had helped shaped the culture of his corporation.

Christians among leaders of other corporations did not all agree with the position taken by this particular executive. It is fruitful to speculate on what specifically Christian, but contrasting, norms the parties to such an intrareligious corporate discussion might have invoked. There would surely be great debate over the "for whose benefit" question. Stockholders suffered from this decision, and some corporate leaders will say that moral and legal responsibility to the interest of stockholders should not have been set aside in subordination to moral concern for people on the other side of the world, especially given (a) the uncertainty of the mixture of benefits and harms resulting from the decision, (b) the impossibility of doing anything in an evil situation which is wholly beneficial, and (c) the virtual certainty that some other company somewhere would take up the turned-down contract.

Remembering that this hypothetical discussion is among professing Christians, one can wonder what references, if any, to the Bible might have cropped up. Would anyone have repeated the Biblical warning (as does Krueger) against idolatry of wealth? Might someone have quoted Jesus, "You cannot serve God and mammon"(Matthew 6:24)? Would anyone have urged that the powers of governments and corporations in South Africa tempt the power holders to benefit from their monopolies in ways analogous to the exploitation of small farmers by the grain merchants against whom the prophet Amos railed (Amos 8:4-6)? Would anyone have pondered out loud what it means theologically for Christians to "live in hope"(Romans 15:13), or what Desmond Tutu meant when, in the 1980s, he said: "In South

Africa it is impossible to be optimistic; therefore it is necessary to hope"?

In fact such discussion is not wholly imaginary, for serious Christians do talk this way to each other. When they participate in the affairs of a business corporation, however, they have to confront myriad forms of the question: How are Christians to relate to people, projects, systems, and policies which have no explicit relation to the historical norms of Christian faith and ethics? The problem, of course, is twofold: (1) What are those norms (a question in perennial dispute among the faithful)? (2) What relation must we seek to other, different norms and their promoters (the question uppermost in H. Richard Niebuhr's typological ordering of historic ways in which Christians have related "Christ and culture")?

David Krueger, himself a serious Christian, has addressed this twofold problem indirectly in his crafting of the master norm of "pursuit of the common good" and his five specific norms for judging the service of a corporation to that common human good. Each of the five bears traces of a biblical tradition that (a) values the material world but refuses to idolize it, (b) measures the good or evil of wealth by its service to genuine human need and especially to the needs of the poor, (c) excludes all versions of "justice" that benefit some through exploitation of others, (d) restrains the sinful proclivities, the self-serving preferences of powerful people, by countering their power with countervailing restraints, and (e) respects the wide world of creation as belonging first to the Creator and then to all creatures great and small. So stated, however, Krueger's five principles take on a more distinctly theological, biblical cast than the forms in which he states them. In my restatements, they may have an uneasy place in the intracorporate board room but may be more at home in those church discussions where Christians feel free to urge biblical traditions of faith and ethics.

Thus, in trying to assess Krueger's position, both he and I have to grapple with the "Christ and culture" debate inside our own minds, in our respective religious communities, and between those communities and the world of corporate cultures. His positive, normatively disciplined perspectives on that latter world are forceful, comprehensive, and timely. In the past two hundred years Americans have moved from an economy in which 90 percent of us worked for ourselves to a society in which less than 10 percent of us do so. From the time of the Civil War on, the leaders of newly formed

102

corporations called upon Americans to adopt the "cooperative" spirit. Most of the world's work from now on, they urged against the ingrained individualism of our culture, will be done in organizations. In spite of the continuation of a strong individualistic evangelical religion in the nineteenth century and its rebirth in recent decades of the twentieth, we are, most of us, organizational men and women.

A strong "Christ against culture" stance in regard to corporate business would lead one to dismiss it religiously as a work of evil spirits. Krueger and I agree that our vocation as Christians does not necessarily entail such an interpretation of what it means to be "in the world but not of the world" (John 18:36). One suspects that in America of the 1990s, there is enough anxiety about the economic future of the country, its businesses, and its jobs that only too many of us Christians are simply grateful to have any well-paying job. In that feeling we are like most of our neighbors. Rather than identifying this stance as "Christ of culture," we might adduce another Niebuhr-like type: Christ in parallel to culture. One might tag it "the island theory." As Niebuhr himself frequently pointed out, the natural theological condition of most of us is a practical form of henotheism: let each compartment of our lives be governed by its own god, and don't worry about building bridges of meaning between the islands. How are Christians to protect themselves and each other from henotheism, that easy, tolerant form of idolatry?

As a further contribution to an answer, I have two major criticisms of the dialogue on economic ethics that Krueger has ably advanced in these chapters, along with two aspirations implicit in the criticisms: (1) To what extent are these rules for corporate ethics in a globalizing economy *biblically warranted*? (2) What happens to these principles when one shifts the context to specific business practices within a capitalistic system as they affect the world's poor?

In sum, I wish there were more wrestling with the Bible in Krueger's essay, and I could wish for more wrestling with the perplexities and conflicts among principles that come with contemporary study of business cases. At work here, doubtless, are differences of temperament and experience that beset the work of any two ethicists. Not to demur before the onslaught of the post-modernist relativists is overidingly important here: I incline to agree with Krueger and others that one cultural threat looming on the horizon of the twenty-first century is the collapse of meaning-systems worldwide—the ordinary province of religion. This is to carry the island mentality to its ultimate individualistic absurdity—to the abandonment of socially relevant ethical consensus altogether.

For the formation of an ethic protected against the acids of relativism, we who seek proper ethical guidelines for our collective behavior may need to delay that search temporarily while we reconnoiter the rooted depths of our religious faiths. Establishing ethics in complete independence of an overarching religious faith (as Kant tried to do) has not been a very fruitful project in modern civilization. Practical ethics without religious roots may be very impractical. The psychologist Kurt Lewin remarked once that "nothing is so practical as a good theory," a remark strictly pertinent to that management discussion of a fifty-million-dollar engine contract: eliminate the moral theory that apartheid was evil and that organizations must seek to restrain evil, and the discussion might have been quickly terminated. Eliminate the religious conviction behind that ethical theory, and the latter may have little staying power. I think of a Korean friend who remarked: "If you have a cause, you might pursue it for several years. If you have an ideology, maybe ten or fifteen. But if you have a faith, you can follow it until you lay down your life."

As it happens, the importance of theory—or assumption—erupts in the face of many a conflict in politics and economics, as all those advocates know who want to downgrade or eliminate *multiplicity* of principles in either ethical theory or business practice. Krueger's five principles are a clear illustration of what Sir Geoffrey Vickers (a British civil servant) called "multivalued choice," a form of choosing that has to be practiced by every politician who acknowledges multiple human interests at stake in lawmaking, every business leader who knows that no human organization lives by financial profit alone, and every ethicist who fights against relativism in claims like: "Our ethics are too diverse to yield a single principle for our social behavior, but we have to agree on at least a cluster of general truths about how we *ought* to behave."

In response to my own rumination here, in what follows I will pursue my two species of uneasiness about Krueger's exposition—the biblical basis of his argument, and the empirical issue of who is winning and who is losing in current trends in this emerging global economy.

A Biblical Context

William Temple once remarked that Christianity is the most materialistic of world religions. Its roots in Israel's exodus from Egypt, and its faith in the incarnate presence of God in human history in Jesus of Nazareth, link the divine and the human in ways that Christians are still trying to understand. Against many an internal heresy and external rival religious view, the Christian movement has sought to steer clear of any theology that denies the enduring value of humanity's material existence; that dismisses some part of human life as unrelated to the will, the judgment, and the redeeming love of God; that either ignores, or despairs over, the reality of sin and evil in human persons and societies; that diminishes the right of any human to be considered a child of God; or that ranks any human "creation" with the perfections of a divine creation still unfolding toward a destination "above all we ask or think."

The positive claims and negative implications in this Christian creed have deep roots in the Hebrew Bible. It is plain in his teachings that Jesus means his followers to be diligent students of "the law and the prophets." It would be healthy in the American Christian churches if collectively we read the Bible diligently enough to be deeply *perplexed* by the problem of what relation, if any, can exist between an ethic associated with a religion taught two and three millennia ago and an ethic suitable to a capitalist global economy. Perplexity is not an exciting or satisfying mental condition, but any claim by modern Christians to be disciples of the biblical word would have a richer integrity if they asked each other more often questions like these:

- Why did the tradition of Israel's liberation from Egyptian slavery so pervasively shape the spirit and the substance of so many laws of the Mosaic tradition relating to economic transactions?

- Why the Torah's tender conscience regarding the needs of "strangers in the land"? (Cf. Exodus 12:49, 18:22-23, Deuteronomy 10:18-19) Why were prosperous farmers required to leave some of their crops for harvesting by the poor and destitute?

- Why the suspicion of interest on loans, a suspicion installed in the first 1,500 years of economic teaching by the subsequent Christian churches?

- What justified the prophet Amos' deep suspicion of the "buy cheap and sell dear" transactions of Bethel grain merchants (8:4-6), and what does this Amos version of "injustice" say about the alleged justice of prices set by markets?

- Since various prophets from Amos to Jeremiah envisioned a great economic future of overflowing economic abundance (Amos 9:13-15, Jeremiah 33:10-13), what forms of repentance and social change did they apparently see as preconditions of the coming of that abundance?

- What is the *spiritual* meaning of the apparent echo, in Jesus' teaching, of the prophets' suspicion of the *wealthy* (Matthew 19:23-24)? What are modern Christians to make of his teachings regarding the instruction to one rich man, "Sell all you have and give to the poor" (Luke 18:23), or his interchange with the tax-profiteer Zaccheus (Luke 19:1-10), or his parable of the barn-builder who accumulated much wealth and "lost his soul"(Luke 12:13-21)? How did issues of wealth and property ever become, for Jesus, issues of heaven and hell (Luke 16:25)? And why all those spiritual contrasts between the rich and the poor in the teachings as recorded in Luke (6:20-21, 24-25)?

Down through the centuries, Christian theologians and others, responding to these themes in the teachings of the biblical tradition, have pondered the difficulties of putting such teachings into practice in the context of radically different economic and social cultures. Perhaps the easiest intellectual exercise is to catalogue the differences: What kinship can there be between the subsistence economy of the first-century Roman world and the industrial-corporate global market economy of the twenty-first century? What can it mean to "seek first the kingdom of God" on the floor of the New York Stock Exchange or in a corporate board deciding to move a computer operation from California to Bangalore? It is a long historical way from a hillside where the Nazarene taught his disciples to lay aside their economic anxieties (Matthew 6:28) and the prospect that your California job is fleeing to India. Of what relevance is that ancient religious-ethical tradition to this unprecedented global economy?

The answer to this question is not easy. I am inclined to say that

David Krueger makes the answer, in theological-biblical terms, too easy. Granted, his choice of the "Christ transforming culture" model of ethical stances, as proposed by H. Richard Niebuhr, concurs with the preference of many others among Niebuhr's readers, including myself. But what is the identity of this Christ who has the power to transform corporate culture? What is the difference, concretely, between the Transformer and the thing being transformed? There are two poles in this model, and somehow the content of the first pole is indistinctly filled out here with the thrusts of those ancient Hebrew and Christian teachings.

A recent (1996) book by three theological ethicists, for example, pays tribute to the wide influence of the fivefold Niebuhr typology of ways Christians have historically related the two poles.[1] These authors, too, take Niebuhr to task for avoiding a certain density of dependence on Jesus' teachings and for minimizing their collision with many a practice in the ordinary lives of contemporary Christians. Appropriating the work of certain recent biblical scholars, for example, the three writers identify seven "bedrock normative practices . . . clearly emphasized by the concretely incarnate Jesus." The first two of these practices would be enough to trouble anyone in 1997 seeking to relate it harmoniously to work in the modern business corporation: "(1) Not judging, but forgiving, healing, and breaking down barriers that marginalize or exclude. . . . (2) Delivering justice: not hoarding money greedily, but giving alms, forgiving debts, breaking bread in the common meal, feeding the hungry, announcing good news for the poor, sharing goods, investing money in God's reign and God's delivering justice." The New Testament references for this summary include Luke 6:34 ("Do good, and lend, expecting nothing in return, and your reward will be great.") and three parables (Matthew 20:1-16, Luke 16:1-31, and Luke 19:11-27) which have furnished classic theological grist for intense discussion between modern Christians inclined to celebrate capitalism and others inclined to condemn it. There follows, in the same Luke 16, the fearful parable of the rich man and Lazarus, the most striking instance in which Jesus makes the choice between economic generosity and economic greed into a choice between heaven and hell.

My aspiration for the thinking of modern day Christians about economic ethics goes beyond the scope of the Krueger essay: namely, that, without falling into an agnostic stance ("who knows what God wills for global economics?") and without blithe theological celebration of the system that has currently scored a victory over its major rival ("God must be on the side of capitalism, for look what's happened to the socialists"), we sit *under* the instructions of the biblical narrative long enough, faithfully enough, to sense anew how profoundly it calls all our economic systems into question, both in their kinship and in their antagonism.

An old ironic observation about Marxists and capitalists, for example, is that they both tend toward a materialism that does tempt their adherents to "live by bread alone" (Luke 4:4). Each is devoted to virtually unlimited accumulation of industrialized wealth. Each allocates great authority to those who, presumably, know best how to manage that wealth: on the one side, the boards and CEOs who govern corporations, and on the other, the Party and the planners of centralized government. Krueger is on strong ground, with Adam Smith, when he discerns that decentralized power in a competitive market system, like the separation of powers in democracy, is a kind of protection against overweening market power. One might say that anti-trust laws are a secular reflection of what it takes to protect economic society from idolatry. But will countervailing intra- and extra-market powers protect any of us, either personally or collectively, from the worship of wealth? One of the great contemporary brakes upon the dream of infinitely expanding global wealth is the wisdom of modern ecology, reminding us scientifically that we do not live by economic production alone but by the oxygen, the soils, the waters, and the other resources of earth. We are enclosed by a "global economy" more ancient than any we have invented and more necessary to our own economic efforts than we sometimes remember. It is as though the earth itself were saying to modern economic pursuers of wealth: "Observe the limits, or lose the blessings of life."

At the very least, this first response to Krueger's well-argued essay is such a word, uttered, I believe, in and through the biblical tradition: "Pursue true riches, and do not fall into the traps of the false." (Cf. Luke 16:11) Churches and other interpreters of this religious heritage should help their adherents to discern the difference between true and false human fulfillment. Krueger and I agree that it is not the chief end of the business corporation to fill all the needs of its employees or its customers. The longer hours we work to "make ends meet" the more we need to know what it means to serve the truly "chief end" of human life, as the old Calvinist formulation put it: "to glorify God and enjoy God forever." To this formulation one might well add an essential biblical complement—"to enjoy the love of your neighbor."

That is why no simple commendation of "more wealth rather than less" will suit the needs and wishes of the global rich or the global poor. Macro-economic growth is an insufficient measure of the humanity of any economic system. An eminently successful Christian business leader in West Berlin, for example, has recently observed that socialist East Germany was "a society of penurious equality." But, he continued, in that society there also existed

> a culture of togetherness, of solidarity among the little people. Life in the GDR [the former German Democratic Republic] was more strenuous because of the effort it took to get hold of many articles of everyday life. Yet at the same time the pace of life was slower. Those without a telephone tend to write letters. House music, reading, theater visits, the garden plot, the bartering of scarce commodities, repairing one's own car or the cars of friends, helping out in the family or circle of friends, neighborliness: great value was attached to all these activities.[2]

Such activities now get overridden among many of those from the former East Germany who are now forced to learn the ways of competition and productive justice. But the tradeoff, many testify, is not trivial or easy. There was some humanity in those forty years of socialism, as well as much oppression. And among the values now being lost are those human relationships that a competitive economy often destroys—as when a new job takes a family member far away or a closed plant devastates an entire local community.

One great moral weakness of capitalist culture, especially from the vantage point of its investors, is that it discriminates very little between what products will profit the business financially and what will benefit customers humanly. The system *itself* makes this discrimination difficult. "If we can sell it, we ought to produce it" is the principle always waiting to dominate boardroom policy making, especially in the anxious competitive environment that destroys overnight the profitability of many a strong enterprise. Ethical conviction can be a fragile protection against fickle investors who look at quarterly reports more eagerly than at the serviceability of products to human need and ecological safety. One fine day, perhaps, when the basic survival needs of all people have been met by market supply and demand, it may be time enough to celebrate the fact that luxury for some in the system supplies a survival income for others. But on the way to such a vision, huge inequalities multiply on a worldwide scale, and the hope of whole generations for even that survival income may get put on indefinite "hold." This is to say that, on the way to increased affluence for the human world as a whole, the ethical problem of economic inequality must not be put on hold. Krueger himself suspects that ecological pressures alone will mandate the permanence of much inequality among the peoples of the next century. The pressures of growing wealth may have to be resisted if the blessing of even moderate prosperity is to fall upon future generations of earth-dwellers. The capitalist system is not well suited for attention to such predictions. Sensitive as they are to mobile capital flows, few corporate managers are protected from a rush to short-term profits. They are unlikely promoters of global systems of control for the *long-range* "common good." In spite of the increase of a sense of corporate social responsibility in many, especially American corporations, the current tendency, in 1997, has been to draw back from ambitious long-range social spinoffs of corporate action, to downsize as need be for profitable survival.

Real human beings are beneficiaries and casualties of this dominance of profitability among the multiple values that clamor for entry in corporate decision making. Love of one's neighbor "as oneself" and special attention to the needs of the world's poor are priorities easily orphaned in these deliberations. Especially orphaned—and Krueger seems to consent to the orphaning—is focused concern for distributive justice. Against the above biblical background, I am bound to protest his easy exclusion of that version of justice from the debate.

Justice for Whom?

As the biophysical limits of earth impose limits on wise human exploitation of earth's resources, so the norm of justice imposes limits on the benefits that any person should derive from relations with another. The ancient formulation, "to each their own," has always begged for specifications of what anyone can rightly count as his or her own, so that struggles over the most appropriate norm of justice have classically moved along two paths: justice in exchange and justice in distribution. To these, I want not only to add a concept of productive justice, but to apply also a reminder that other parts of the tradition have added both contributive and retributive justice—"you get back what you give out." In this discussion, I want to focus, above all, on implications of "contributive justice."

The Marxian motto—"From each according to ability and to each according to need"—combines the two major forms. A market economy has the democratic advantage of giving individuals the right to define their own needs and to use their purchasing powers accordingly. To put it simply: to enjoy the "free market" one has to possess money. Since that requirement is scantily fulfilled for some people in every society, advocates of distributive justice have never lacked for reason to cry out: "Markets ignore the needs of the neediest!" They characteristically call for a justice named compensatory or restorative.

A rational division between the two types seems rather alien to the thought world of the Bible. Norman Snaith once observed that in ancient Hebrew, the word for "justice" is always "toppling over" into kinship with the word for "mercy." More recently, Ronald Marstin has suggested that "justice is a matter of who and what we can tolerate neglecting."[3] The two observations should remind any Bible-reader that the Hebrew ethic, voiced especially in the prophets, had a low tolerance for neglecting the weak, the vulnerable, and marginal folk of their society. Their normative preference for compensatory and restorative forms of justice we may want to call "charity," but the paternalism in the modern use of that word does not fit the prophetic usage. Remembering the deliverance from Egyptian slavery, the prophets were always reminding their fellow citizens that their society was founded, not on a rational exchange of mutual benefit, but on a covenant initiated as a transforming divine gift.

In any search for some conformity with the Hebrew and Christian tradition here, a modern theological ethic for economic life will either take seriously the surmise, "We are more receivers than givers," or it will lean philosophically towards the master rule, "You get what you contribute." This is not far from a motto fitting some aspects of Krueger's definition of productive justice, which could be considered as a fresh formulation of contributive justice and one of the most valuable dimensions of his analysis. "Something for nothing" seems ill-adapted to the world of economic exchanges, and even the marketing claim "more for your money" leans toward rough balances between what one gives and what one gets.

H. Richard Niebuhr used to recommend to his students the rule, "Thinkers are more likely to be right in what they affirm than in what they deny." Krueger's dismissal of liberation theology's preference for distributive justice and its restorative and compensatory forms is much too casual. He should argue less with Gutierrez and Cone, more with the Bible. And, in the modern particular, he should be worried by the enormous dislocations of workers from jobs and the equally enormous disparities between the incomes of who is winning and who is losing in the current shifts of income domestically in the United States.

At various points Krueger appeals to the work of the other Niebuhr, Reinhold. One of that Niebuhr's favorite anecdotes, born of the economic distresses of the 1930s, concerned a group of orphanage trustees who approached the president of an ailing factory with a request that he join the board of the orphanage. Looking out of the window at the factory buildings, the executive said sadly, "This morning I fired fifty men. Some of their children may end up soon in your orphanage. You do not want a man like me on your board."

The end of the story was that the visitors replied, "No, you are exactly the sort of man we want. You feel burdened by these very griefs." Niebuhr's point was that an ideal of justice, seemingly impossible in the immediate situation, was still indispensable to genuine moral conscience. Better to feel guilt under the authority of an "impossible ideal" than blithely to plead "the market made me do it." For the sake of corporate survival, the market does occasionally push toward downsizing for heightening efficiency. At minimum it is right to ask how executives and their boards *feel* about this apparent necessity. As someone who has himself had to fire people in a seminary faced with financial stringencies, I empathize with all those executives who say that firing people is the most painful occasional duty of their job. I am less empathetic with those who excuse themselves by economic necessity, and I am deeply antagonistic to the policy that *rewards* managers for their courage in firing people. To be sure, a guilty conscience can be a bad substitute for the remedial behavior that a pragmatic ethic surely requires: All credit to those companies like IBM who undertake elaborate help to its soon-to-be-dismissed employees in finding them new jobs. But more credit yet to those who put into practice two other tactics in relation to the plight of men and women thrown out of work: sharing their pain in the form of refusing raises and bonuses throughout the company and lobbying government or other outside agencies to provide the jobs that the corporation is no longer able to supply.

I find no studied attention to such tactics in what Krueger has written here, which is consistent with his neglect of distributive justice. Most observers of the post-1980 business climate in the United States testify that vigor in pursuit of corporate survival has overtaken vigor of loyalty between workers and employers, with the result that a U.S. Steel company, moving in the decade 1985–1995 from 120,000 employees to 20,000 and to a new competitive position in the world market, is the object of much congratulation in executive and economist circles. Not many voices in *those* circles rise to criticize the executives and boards who reward each other with large multi-million dollar bonuses for these alleged achievements. Granted, it takes determination to fire some people for the survival benefit of others; but the disparity between the pain and the reward in these transactions should evoke some very basic ethical protest. It is hard to see, in Krueger's dependence on something like the natural laws of global markets, room for this protest. We should admire the small steel company in South Carolina that survived the virtual collapse of the American industry by a policy of shared profit and loss among all the employees of the company, including top executives. Japanese companies have long followed the same practice. It may not be the master key to corporate survival (even Japanese companies are retreating from life-tenure for their employees), but it is surely a key to company *morale*, which is only a letter away from *moral*.

The author of Psalm 15 defined righteous people as those who "swear to their own hurt" (Ps. 15:4), a principle at work in Reinhold Niebuhr's guilty executive and his kin among downsizers who refuse colossal financial rewards for their decisions. The principle is a good one for those Christian writers, like me, who urge fellow Christians to worry about neighbors—some of them middle class—losing out in current explosions of the global marketplace. In late 1996 a *New York Times* editorial noted that 1995 and 1996 were years of relative improvement in the incomes of the most vulnerable Americans. Poverty among African Americans was back to its 1959 rate (29.3 percent), child poverty was on the decrease, and income inequality was back to a late 1960s level, largely because the number of jobs in an upbeat economy were increasing. Was this "progress"? Not necessarily, notes the *Times:*

The recent gains, though welcome, ought to be kept in perspective. Poverty would have to fall four more years at last year's rate just to reach the level that was achieved 23 years ago. Black poverty last year, the lowest in recorded history, remains far worse than white poverty. Family incomes are rising, but remain below 1989 levels for all but the richest. Inequality has fallen for two years, but the average income of families in the bottom 20 percent is only one-twentieth as high as the average income of families in the top 5 percent. Child poverty remains at an obscenely high 20 percent.

The editorial goes on to say that the 1996 "reform" of the Federal welfare program is almost certain to worsen these statistics: "Just as the economy opens the door to prosperity for families, rich and poor, Congress has slammed the door back shut for the most disadvantaged."[4]

Not to be forgotten here are the rewards experienced in 1996 by the most advantaged—the growth in average American corporative executive compensation from about 50 times that of their lowest paid workers to 250 times that of the lowest. One could record such facts with a serene composure, of course: "The market works out that way." To write with a mixture of serenity and disturbance, however, one must be a celebrator of both productive and distributive justice. Equal poverty does not make a society just; neither does unequal affluence.

Advocates of productive justice may argue for these discrepancies in terms of the survival of profitable corporations. They may thus go to sleep comfortably at night. But such comfort is ethically ill-advised, unless one wants to take one's clues for ethics from other books than the Bible and from utilitarian economic ideologies that mostly celebrate the survival of the fittest and the greatest good of the greatest number. It is worth remembering here that the acid test of a democracy is not majority rule but minority protection: a test profoundly compatible with Leviticus 19 and Deuteronomy 26, not to speak of Matthew 25.

But there is a problem with my advocacy here, and doubtless Krueger would be the first to point it out. One dimension of his economic vision, close to that of the Bible, is the hope that grinding poverty may be eliminated from the human world and that business enterprise can be the instrument of this hope in ways that neither socialist nor liberal economies have been able to achieve in the twentieth century. In this, Krueger shares a principal aim of the liberation theologians. Their faith in socialism formally matches his in capitalism. That both may be faulty servants of the world's poor is a possibility that needs more attention, in this writer's opinion. May it not be that every economic system, like every political system, has it distinctive weaknesses and vulnerability to injustice and even to tragedy? Are not Bible-reading Christians and Jews obligated to be alert to folk most damaged by the working of any economic system?

Even aside from that critical perspective, however, our late-century global marketplace is benefiting certain previously poor populations in certain world regions, and a genuine concern for the deliverance of *all* humanity from poverty has to welcome this fact. The sense of crisis among Americans here stems from real losses to our national economy and real gains to some millions of workers around the world. Even if we admit that global economics is not a zero-sum game, that the dynamics of free trade and comparative productive advantages have international benefits, the troubling fact for Americans is that their 50 percent of international trade in 1950 has shrunk now to 25 percent. Some of the gain to workers abroad has been bought at the expense of more than a few Americans.

What must Christian ethics make of this development? A generation ago theologians related to the World Council of Churches advocated a transfer of wealth from the rich industrial west to the poorer countries of Africa and Asia. Now, ironically, thanks to vast new devices for international capital mobilization and investment, some such capital transfers are now taking place. We may rightly protest, in the name of distributive justice, that income and wealth disparities have become just as skewed (or more so) in the developing countries as in the United States. But the facts remain: Americans as a whole are not getting richer at the rate of a generation ago. Some Americans are benefiting from the new global competition; but some millions of us have lost jobs and incomes in the wake of industries that have moved to Mexico, Indonesia, and Taiwan.

What advocate of justice for the world's poor can, in good faith, protest this development? Even if their incomes were to be frozen at 1996 levels, Americans would still be the richest people on earth. In the name of the justice that I have promoted here, ought we not to "swear to our own hurt" and acknowledge that the mass of the world's poor deserve a *lot* of benefit at our expense? Either from a perspective purely ethical or one purely capitalist (one thinks of Joseph Schumpeter's "creative destruction" of the uncompetitive enterprise), are we not drawn reluctantly to the conclusion that the global market, by fits and lurches, is growing more just?

We know that such a claim has almost no political appeal in any rich country, and we can be almost certain that American politicians in the twenty-first century will continue to talk about keeping this country the richest and most powerful in the world. It is less certain, however, that America's business leaders can be counted on to talk this way without hypocrisy. Multinational corporations are creatures of diminished patriotism as their leaders attend to productive efficiency, profits, and capital transfers on a world scale. They value overall economic growth of the corporation and the world system, including the growth among the world's poor. They may not be heartless about the loss of jobs to their home countries, but they are not shy about saying to the religious proponents of economic justice for the poor: "You asked for it, and we are getting it—only not necessarily in your particular country."

This is not an easy argument for liberation theologians, or their socialist and liberal friends, to answer. Socialism has probably made more humane contributions to the poor of many Western and East European countries than the triumphalist spirit of neocapitalists likes to allow. An illustration would be the improvement of health among Cubans during the Castro regime. Now, however, the promise and peril of global economics is beginning to reach deep into the lives of people across the global class spectrum. Thrown into ambiguity, for critics like myself, is every easy answer to the ancient questions, "Who is my neighbor?" and "Benefit for whom?" How can we answer with a blithe "every human being" when the family next door has just lost half of its income? Shall we shift our understanding of the parable of the good Samaritan to focus on that near-at-hand neighbor, so that we willingly restrict our ethical concern to that neighbor, and offer our congratulations to those businesses and political parties who care for American economic interests above all others?

I have a pair of very sober responses to my own questions here. First, Christians among Americans should celebrate the diminishment of poverty in any country and should demand of managers and investors policies that push governments and economic elites everywhere toward at least Krueger's standard of productive justice. Entailed in such a stance would be alertness to the ancient temptations of exploitative profits from the labor of poor people who are willing to work for any wage that their market will bear. In 1996, for example, the Disney Corporation was paying clothing workers in Haiti fifteen cents an hour. Even by Haitian standards this was half of a survival income, but the market result was cheaper clothes for North Americans.

Our concern for justice for the world's poor must be matched, secondly, by equal concern for justice for poor Americans. Precisely because we are a very rich country, our attention to justice inside our borders should climb to the top of ethical priority. If and when recession comes, that priority becomes the more urgent.

And this brings one back to the missing dimension of Krueger's analysis of the distribution of rewards inside the corporation itself. Among all its constituents, who are lions deserving the lions' share? In his criticism of socialist systems, he fails to note that modern socialists, even those that were proudly communist, have never invoked absolute equality as the only form of economic justice. Soviet and Chinese political leaders have never hesitated to claim incomes twice as high as that of the factory worker, and we know that their actual income ratios, fattened by perquisites, have been quite in excess of 2:1. Communist Yugoslavia, in fact, tolerated an official ratio of 5:1, a remarkable concession to contributive justice for an economic-political theory based on the principle, "From each according to ability, to each according to need." The assumption in the socialist countries seems to be: some people do contribute more, and they deserve more economic reward.

But how much more? Two recent articles from the *New York Times* represent the kind of question I am posing. One reports the study of seventy-six executives, more than seventy of whom were paid more than one million dollars per year. It cites Richard Freedman, the Harvard labor economist, who points out that a 30:1 ratio in the 1960s rose to more than 100:1 in 1995. Further, in the years between 1993 and 1995, stock values rose a total of 36 percent, but the stock options of these CEOs rose 125 percent. Rises like these, according to Paula Todd of the Towers Perrin consulting firm, escalate the expectations of all those in higher management. And the second, more recent article documents that the spread continues to increase. Not only does the percent of GNP gained by the families in the bottom fifth of the population continue to decline, from 5.4 percent in 1970 to 4.2 percent in 1994, but the top five percent of the population got a greater share, from 15.6 percent to 20.1 percent. "And it is still true that corporate CEOs . . . now make 120 times as much or more (as employees)."

Capitalism's exclusion of the question from serious attention is

not entirely duplicated by Krueger here, but neither does he adequately clarify the measure of "how much." He does nod to justice-
as-need in his hope for the lifting of the world's poor out of grinding
poverty, and he is tolerant enough of a minimum wage law enforced
by government. But it is hard to argue for that latter law from the
facts of market economics and the principle of productive justice.
Typically business managers seek low labor costs and the pegging of
hourly wages at levels acceptable to people of the required compe-
tence. Wage justice is a matter of supply and demand, and only by
recourse to some justice principle other than contribution is any
investor likely to agree to a minimum wage law. "Pay what a worker
needs to survive in this society" is such a recourse, a specification of
a justice-in-distribution whose negative form is: "It is unjust for some
workers to starve while others in the enterprise are feasting."

I have yet to meet a business manager who, in behavior if not in
speech, could so consistently promote contributive justice that no
other form of justice had even an implicit place in his or her affirmation of market-oriented ethics. I remember well a discussion among
textile executives in North Carolina in which one of them, a proud
advocate of market competition, looked around the table and said,
"We are in the business of putting each other out of business if we
can." Efficiency for competitive dominance was his motto. Later in
the same hour, however, the discussion turned to the question of
what to do with a superannuated employee with no pension who
was no longer an efficient factory worker. "Why not fire him?" I
asked. "Well," came the reluctant answer, "we didn't have the heart
to throw him out."

Students of the textile industry will recognize the echo of paternalism in that answer, but students of the Bible should recognize as
well a troubled turn toward compassion-for-need as a necessary
ingredient of almost *any* discussion of justice that even faintly echoes
the biblical use of the term. The most generous judgment I can make
of Krueger's dismissal of ethical concentration upon distributive
justice is that he is not ready to jettison the concept altogether; he
simply believes that Marxist ideologues and liberation theologians
have neglected the proper normative and empirical priority of contributive justice for the creation of wealth.

I have purposefully termed all of us who participate in productive enterprises as "workers," avoiding if I can a strict division between those who work, those who manage, and those who profit. I

would cheerfully advance the New Testament image of the church—one body with members of diverse and indispensable gifts—as an image of a humane organization in which each member "has the same care for the other" (1 Corinthians 12:25) and has work to do for the sake of the "common good" (12:8). All are workers, all are valuable. Steep hierarchical pyramids of reward are out of bounds in this image. For Christians who believe that their religious communities are meant to embody an ethic, and forms of human relationship, that are clues to the content of the "Christ" that is to transform "culture," this is no trivial analogy. Ethically suggestive analogy from church to other forms of human society has some powerful precedent in the history of Christian ethics, especially in Reformed Protestantism.

Not long ago, a Russian leader of his country's new human rights movement, answered my question, "Why did Communism fail economically?" with the answer: "Because we had no reason to work hard, and because we had poor management." Krueger and other apologists for global capitalism should find this a confirming word from a person who grew up under communism. Contributive justice seems to fit a certain fact about human nature: we are indeed motivated by rewards, and getting the same wage for working twice as hard as somebody else eventually strikes us as unjust.

Jesus was fully aware of this fact when he told his parable of the laborers in the vineyard, whose employer paid the same wage to all workers regardless of how many hours each worked (Matthew 20:1-16). In a contrasting parable (Luke 19:11-27) he seemed to acknowledge the justice of diligent "putting money to work" through investment. The one parable images the generous justice of God, the other the divine imperative of personal stewardship.Strictly economic arguments based on either or both of these parables may be perilous, but it is hard not to see in the first a dominant theme in the New Testament account of the Christian life: "By grace you have been saved through faith, and this is not your own doing, it is the gift of God" (Ephesians 2:8). And in the second: "You must work out your own salvation in fear and trembling; for it is God who works in you . . ." (Philippians 2:12-13). How to weave these two themes into the fabric of an economic ethic deserving the name Christian, may not yet be clearly known among Christians worldwide. But these have to be the terms of our part in the discussion. In *starting* from this root lies our hope for making a distinctive contribution to next century's ongoing human dialogue about economic justice.

Chapter 3

A Plea for Viable Entry Points in Debates on Economic Justice

Laura L. Nash

"The sad face of the man who has too much work of one kind is only equaled by the worried face of a man out of a job."
—Percival Wicksell[1]

No doubt the conditions of a modern economy have created a kind of work that causes both the winners and the losers to suffer profoundly. Many of the losers in the global economic balance seem eternally condemned to life in the poverty trap, while the winners experience all the psychological and social anxieties associated with a state of anomie. Thus even in the face of the obvious failure of communism, the question plagues us, is the system of capitalism so inherently flawed in its results as to be immoral? Can this system be justified at a theological or philosophical level?

David Krueger's essay takes up a number of important facets of this question, which I will not insult the reader by repeating in total. Rather, I would like to point out what I see as particularly helpful in his paper, and also suggest that the search for a theologically justifiable economic order must carry the terms of inquiry further than, as he puts it, "the shaping of a normative ethic for business corporations in a global economy."

Krueger makes the important point that there are many reasons for believing that it is possible to justify from a Christian standpoint participation in markets at the local or global level. In following the general post-communist shift of focus to a discussion of productive justice, he suggests that the flawed record of results under free market economies is not a sign of total moral failure, but rather of *incompleted* opportunity to achieve the common good. In this very important shift of perspective, the glass becomes half full. The current predominance of various kinds of capitalism around the world is a sign of progress from an eschatological standpoint. The main question, then, from Krueger's standpoint, is how are Christians to take the measure of progress and thus be in a position to devise better rules and institutions? His adaptation and application of H. Richard Niebuhr's five theological categories offers us a perspective of hope and the moral obligation to recognize the nature of our participation in capitalism's successes as well as its failures. His essay makes the important suggestion that it is right for Christians to be engaged in the search for goals, institutional arrangements and restraints that will in part have as a goal the advancement of free market economic activity.

Rather than addressing this argument on ontological grounds, I would like to ask a slightly different question, to be applied not only to Krueger's argument but to any theoretical moral discussion of the economy: Does the theory sufficiently consider the question of its own execution? Where I strongly differ with him is (1) on the potential contribution that conventional normative expressions can make to the common good and (2) how globalism currently shapes the moral inquiry into the norms of capitalism. In short, I would like to go back to square one and ask what it is we really *need* from a conventional theological justification of capitalism in a global context. In this response I will discuss both the limits of normative theory to serve these needs and the probable impact of globalism. I would suggest that both must be reexamined in order to generate what I would call "viable access points" for the entry of Christian theology into the economic affairs of humankind.

Reassessing the Impact of Globalism

To take up the topic of globalism first, I would like to suggest that there is a widely held and legitimate alternative view to the description of globalism that appears in Krueger's essay—one to which I subscribe. I raise this cautionary note about the differences in our understanding of the world economy not simply to warn readers against making any investments based on the economic judgements they read here, but because our different understanding of the world order leads to profoundly different assessments of whether or not there has been a "historical affirmation" of Christian possibility in the newly ordered global market economy. How we see this question necessarily affects where we will place our hopes for a transformational theology.

Obviously there is a growing global economy, but it is less clear to me who is participating and how. As Pam Woodall, economics editor of *The Economist*, notes, "Many feel that Adam Smith's invisible hand is trying to push them off a cliff."[2] She also feels after reviewing the positions of a number of key economists and political pundits that the *scale* of globalization (and technological change) tends to be vastly exaggerated. I am cautiously reluctant to assume that worldwide capitalism is the inevitable choice of humankind just because Soviet-style communism has failed and no unified counterfoil to capitalism has yet emerged. Communism is nearly defunct, at least for the moment.[3] But for all the alleged inevitability of capitalism, there seems to be a surprisingly large number of Russians, Asians, Americans, Europeans, Africans, and Middle Easterners who favor cartels and organized crime as an economic alternative to the free market.

Clearly the tally on capitalism's universal desirability is still out, as is the form that capitalism will ultimately take in these new markets. Clearly many new entries are not modeling their economies on the democratic, free market principles of the United States, which at the very least calls into question how the theologian makes sense of such basics as access to competition and production in a global marketplace. Many new market economies that might give us hope of a more just worldwide economic order are situated within a political and social milieu that lags far behind the legal and political infrastructures of the West. From Indonesia to Moscow to Mexico, the new markets are being heavily shaped by totalitarian impulses to restrict entry, restrict competition, restrict information, and keep up the political suppression of those within the borders who might pose a competitive threat.

It would be dangerously naive to see the fall of the Soviet bloc as the equivalent of an economic apocalypse wherein capitalism is interpreted to have assumed some natural (even "providential") position. Any such interpretation seems to me to run the risk of repeating the mistakes of many theologians in this century who based their normative political and economic constructions on simplistic ideological portrayals of communism rather than on the quite observable discrepancies between party line and the human condition under a communist government.

I am equally unconvinced that the dismantling of a bipolar geopolitical order has been a step toward worldwide unification. Samuel Huntington's *The Clash of Civilizations and the Remaking of World Order*[4] is to me as plausible as it is disturbing. He makes the argument that while there is less economic distinction between the peoples of the world (from the standpoint of systems, not personal wealth), there is an increasing disharmony of cultures. These "fault lines" between clashing civilizations such as can be seen in Bosnia, Chechnya, Sri Lanka, the Sudan, etc. pose an increasing threat to world peace. If anything, the fall of a bipolar geopolitical order has dispersed one comprehensible enmity into hundreds of little incomprehensible ones, over which the United States or the United Nations have much less control. Huntington assembles a significant host of evidence that suggest we should not rely on a global economic order to overcome these clashes:

> There is an assumption that increased interaction among people—trade, investment, tourism, media, electronic communication generally—is generating a common world culture. Improvements in transportation and communication technology have indeed made it easier and cheaper to move money, goods, people, knowledge, ideas, and images around the world. No doubt exists as to the increased international traffic in these items. Much doubt exists, however, as to the impact of this traffic. Does trade increase or decrease the likelihood of conflict? The assumption that it reduces the probability of war between nations is, at a minimum, not proven, and much evidence exists to the contrary.[5]

It would be hasty to conclude that democratic capitalism will inevitably be the economic system of world choice, and to further conclude that it is thus out of divine governance or emergent natural order. All we can really say is that, with some very notable exceptions, capitalism seems to be the system most capable of motivating people to push themselves to effectively engage in a collective, common effort to produce *something* that will further secure the daily bread of some people. Whether it will work to significantly alleviate poverty in Eastern Europe or India or Africa or Asia over time is an untested hope. Whether it will form the framework for the Christian's personal transformation through vocation is also not clear. Currently capitalism seems to have an inevitable dependency on an ethic of consumption.[6] In the face of increasing personal and community distress over the culture of consumption in the United States, it is not conclusively clear that capitalism can coexist with long term Christian notions of the common good and a transformed self.

In short, we are not necessarily any closer in the long run to a fulfillment of Christian possibility in this world simply because communism has collapsed and market economies are taking hold in all parts of the globe. There is not necessarily a positive correlation between increased global economic extent and a sense of mutual connectedness across cultural boundaries. The British Empire did not bring global peace and prosperity.

Undoubtedly, in many industries the corporation is engaged in the unprecedented creation of global connections for the purposes of production, efficiency, financial risk, and marketing. It is not unusual for a single product to depend on the participation of people in several nations from the time of its design inception to its final sale. Managers must regularly deal with the process of harnessing a new international labor supply, international financial instruments, multiple design sources, widespread distribution channels, and "overseas" consumers. Undoubtedly where there are more competitors there is a greater possibility of influencing product quality and price. Where there is a profit to be made from cooperation, there can be increased motivation to "make things work" across cultural boundaries. This bodes well to the degree that globalism invites widespread participation, but since globalism in practice seems to be inviting even larger concentrations of power, there is a realistic possibility that the new capitalism will lead to new abuses of labor and consumer trust. Meanwhile the panic attack of the American corporation in the face of global competition threatens to create a class of workaholic globe trotters cut off from their families and their local communities.

If there is increasing chaos, fragmentation, and distance between rich and poor in countries where market expansions are occurring, if concentrations of power on a global scale feed a cartelization of markets, and these are enforced by repressive political power, then it is hard to predict the rise of a "global consensus" over capitalism's social benefits. All we can say is that the center of power may be shifting from the historic geographical contours of the nation-state to an as-yet-unknown "virtual center" based on transactional and capital clout. If Fernand Braudel is right,[7] those at the center will inevitably achieve an unfair advantage, and that advantage will have been predicated by capitalism. If Huntington is right, global capitalism's alleged congruence with natural order may imply not so much transcendence but a replay of the age-old return to our more predatory, bestial selves. The connectedness of those inside the power structure will also pave the way for a dissolution of normative cultural restraints on behavior, thereby sowing the seeds for a general disregard of those without power or even preemptive aggression.

Disciplining the Normative

Krueger and I are in agreement that there is a reality of sin at a deep structural level of society that must be confronted even as we entertain the possibility of individual and global transcendence. We disagree, however, on the adequacy of normative theory, as it is conventionally expressed (perhaps especially by professional ethicists), to address the problem of sin as it plays out in the form of economic injustice. If sin is associated with distancing from God, then a reasonable criterion for normative theory would be that it brings us closer to God as individuals and a society. My question here is not over the ontological aspects of Krueger's transformational theology, but rather the path it lays to application. Does the theory sufficiently consider the question of its own execution? Is the development of theory in itself a transformational act?

The applicability question has plagued all normative work in business ethics, but with little effect on the parameters attached to successful theory-building. It is illustrative in this respect to review the progress of the dialogue that Adolf Berle began when he disputed the then popular view that impersonal markets were so dominant and so firmly regulated by self-interest as to render our corporate society without a conscience and without a soul. Berle felt that the role of the manager in mediating between owner and marketplace lead to the creation of a spirit of consensus in the modern corporation's decision-making machinery "which for good or ill is acting surprisingly like a collective soul." Berle, like Krueger, concluded that the time was ripe for corporations to "consciously take account of philosophical considerations. And they must consider the kind of a community in which they have faith, and which they will serve."[8]

Today's emphasis on stakeholder expressions of corporate responsibility—and their attendant more refined forms of the social audit—can be seen as direct descendants of Berle's work.[9] The new call is to "think about" (in normative terms) those who "have a stake" in the outcomes of corporate activity (nearly everybody) in some organized fashion consistent with an approved philosophical or theological value system. The call can hardly be argued from the standpoint of moral intentions. On the other hand, with twenty-five years of Berle mutations and/or of pro-Marxist frameworks from the Christian theologians available in print, it seems imperative that we take a sober look at the outcomes of business ethics theory and theological critiques of capitalism and business to test whether this form of inquiry in its present state leads to any real-world contributions in the form of action or change of attitude that leads to action. One would be tempted to conclude that there is some Doomsday device built into this kind of analysis that actually prevents it from turning into application.

I would like to take up this point here because I fear that globalism will provide just the sort of complexifying idea that will cause the theoreticians to run back to the drawing board for an indefinite period in order to construct more theories for business consumption, and that any actual application of those theories will thus be further delayed. Krueger has already run to the drawing board and constructed a respectable theory (one which Shriver challenges at predictable points). Assuming it will be a model for further inquiry, I would like at this junction to question whether the framing of normative guidelines and theological justification is time well spent unless it provides a realistic window to application, now, as part of the theory. I would call this window an entry point for the interface of the Christian view and the conduct of business. For the theory-builder, it is a call for a moral viability test on the theory itself.

Krueger suggests topics for application by posing a number of important ethical choices concerning business policy: should a company conduct business with a very corrupt or oppressive political regime? Should shareholders support a tobacco company? He suggests that an adoption of restraints in these areas should be interpreted as a "Christ against culture" stand. To the degree that he offers a religiously anchored explanation of this choice, he has contributed an important new sense of dimension to the business decision. Once on the theological radar screen, the decision then has the potential to be tested for its contribution to the transformation of culture into, well, I'm not sure what, but something closer to God's design of goodness.

What does this approach say about the *role* of religion in business? Stated simply, it attempts to place theological authority over pure economic criteria in deciding what is the right thing to do. This approach is a direct response to the conditions first noted by R. H. Tawney concerning the modern economy.[10] In medieval times, economic life was regulated in large part by the authority of the church; in modern times, not at all, until the church recently began exercising its economic power as a consumer and stockholder. There have been many thoughtful critiques of this role both in terms of its "fit" with reality and it's ability to capture essential aspects of the ethical/theological nature of decisions in the business world. Michael Novak notes that many church leaders mistakenly formulate their own sense of role based on that older social order. They see themselves as visionaries, imposing authority from above, within a social framework more like the traditional church than the pluralistic global marketplace.[11]

The older model is inappropriate because in fact the church does not have this authority in the modern world, and if it did, it would immediately confront extreme struggles over authority from various religious bodies in the "global" arena. Economic actors would exhibit even less moral consensus than is now the case. As a simple example, the Roman Catholic head of a pharmaceutical company would no longer be in the birth control business, even if the liberal Protestant vice-president of sales had been told that population reduction was the first best answer to the problem of poverty in India.

Another cause of the failure to connect at anything other than the most simplistic, go or no-go level of understanding is the structure and language of conventional theoretical inquiry. Elegant theoretical justifications are constructed, ideally reflecting the full weight of tradition and the economic facts, though the latter often seem to be naively and incompletely considered. Such constructions are not exactly applied, they are *reduced* to a secularized form of policies and codes in order to be cast in a language familiar to business: just tell me what I can and can't do.

Richard Rorty has warned against the dangers of conducting philosophical or theological inquiry on the model of judicial proceedings.[12] Though he had Kant and Lyotard specifically in mind, the remark is particularly apt for many of the normative models in business ethics, including the one we are considering here. The judicial model, in fixing on the formulation of normative rules and final judgements about application fails to engage the effective messiness that characterizes real actors (John Dewey's "experimentalism"). As such they doom the theory to abandonment or terminal reductionism by real actors. Ronald Green's discussion of the "deep structure" of religion reminds us that the reasoning about this structure, itself filled with paradoxical tensions, has a necessary complexity.[13] How in the face of obvious reductionist tendencies among business people, are these complex discussions to be connected to the thinking and behavior of business people?

Given the decision-oriented bias of most business people, the judicially posed questions are easily subjected to a reductive, trivializing process. It would not be difficult to image a business person engaging the notion of "Christ transforming culture" no more deeply than as an indication that it is permissible to go ahead with his or her plan, with perhaps a few compensatory adjustments, "Christ against culture" would mean a no-go. I will argue in the third part of this essay that the postmodern economic culture cannot responsibly be reduced to this kind of simplicity. Nevertheless, this kind of reduction of theological norm is not only commonplace, it leads to immoral consequences. Unforeseen problems remain unanticipated and unaddressed in the theologian's framing of the business person's choices. A good example is the South Africa divestiture movement of the 1970s and 1980s. What was originally a thoughtful and passionate critique of responsibility regarding apartheid became a list of principles that were quickly reduced to a go/no-go decision. Clergy and religious business people managed to reduce the problem to a choice of divesting or not, with no attention to *how* that divestiture should occur or what meaning between peoples could be created from the action. I would say very little meaning was created among the hard core investment community. Divestiture in many cases was not a moral response, but a market response to a messy shareholder suit. The simplicity of the choice invited many unethical results as divested businesses were picked up by unscrupulous and sometimes racist opportunists, and no ground was laid for a post-apartheid South Africa.[14]

While the loss of a potential to do good is bad enough, the even greater problem in the attempt to apply theory is the loss of awareness of *religious meaning*. To my mind this is the greatest problem in the current religious and ethical dialogue about business: there is no mediating language or framework that captures the special forms of meaning of religion and philosophy in such a way that the economic actor can integrate these meanings into the full complexity of his or her economic activities. I note that the applied questions in Krueger's essay reveal little of their religious origin. Any secular humanist or corporate board of directors worried about performance and reputation would ask the same questions in much the same way.

Not only is there a loss of religious or philosophical meaning in the attempt to apply theory, but the theologian and philosopher often get muddled in their roles as they move to allegedly real examples. They become para-economists, arguing the economic and organizational benefits of this policy or that, or para-managers, weighing the "people problems" rather in the same way any conscientious manager would do, but often with much less knowledge and experience. Those not drawn to the role of para-economist or para-manager take refuge in their theories, leaving the application to others, that is, undone.

In some cases there is a fuller attempt to move to application, but as suggested, significant efforts have been confined chiefly to boycotts, shareholder suits, and the development of codes of conduct. Of all these, the development of that equally normative but less elegant moral commandment, the business ethics code (with its attendant monitoring and training programs) have been the most widespread application of ethical theory in American business. But even here the judicial model of inquiry has predominated to such an extent that most code efforts concentrate on the affirmation or extension of pre-existing legal restraints on competitive behaviors while overlooking the development of specific guidelines in precisely the areas which are most engaging Christian theologians: the distribution of resources concerning production, human rights, and fairness issues. In the context of real corporate activity, universalization of economic theology works as a feeling or intention of goodwill, but hardly as a reality.

While codes have undoubtedly raised an *awareness* of some ethical aspects of corporate behavior, their focus might be said to be notably removed from the key questions of Christian morality such as the nature of one's obligation to the poor, the establishment of God's order, salvation. Instead, codes tend to facilitate application in those areas that promote the interests of the firm (no conflict-of-interest, auditing compliance, use of competitive information). While stakeholder theories have been an attempt to move the discussion beyond these issues to basic questions of justice and fairness,

130

there are few indications that these theories have made an entry into the area of action beyond creating committees and movements to write more codes or hold more conferences and speeches. They may even do harm because they simply "don't compute." Joseph Biancala has suggested that vague notions of justice as exemplified in some stakeholder theories and corporate constituency statutes actually undermine managers' understanding of fiduciary duty by removing the clear adjudicatory constraints.[15]

Take, for example, the issue of productive justice. A wide range of topical applications have been discussed in print although not clearly and precisely under this title; but for all this attention there is a notable lack of progress in U.S. business practice regarding even our own working poor, i.e., those at the bottom end of the wage gap in the United States. At this point in time, there are few sanctions in this area beyond the minimum wage. One occurs at Herman Miller Corporation, where the devout Protestant chairman, Max De Pree, voluntarily put a cap on his own salary and worked out a formula limiting the range between highest and lowest compensation, against the advice of his board of directors. His effort was based on his own biblical understanding of what he call's "God's mix" and obligations to take care of the least advantaged. It is instructive to note that this intrusion of what might conform to Krueger's "Christ Transforming Culture" occurred without benefit of a sustained normative theory, and there has not since been widespread study of De Pree's actions despite the theoretical interest in productive and distributive justice. Given the historic lack of contact between theory and action, one has to question whether a continued effort at framing normative guidelines for relevance to economic decisions will be time well spent.

A continued satisfaction with the idea that anything beyond theory is mere gravy is particularly problematic in the context of creating interpretive Christian guidance for the conduct of capitalism (with the emphasis on conduct). I would take this question especially seriously in light of the globalization phenomenon, for in response to many of the conditions Krueger identifies at the beginning of his essay we already see the familiar dead-end patterns of application occurring: international ethics codes are being advocated as the necessary first step in applying good intentions to excruciatingly bad practices worldwide. Without the provision of real entry points for the engagement of meaning making and community building and behavior change within the companies, such efforts will be truly academic from the standpoint of business action.

These consequences of theory development must be taken seriously if business ethics, or theological comment on business, is to have any legitimacy. The challenge, then, for the theologian, seems to me to be *to provide the entry point for the Christian perspective, however we understand it, and equally important, to effect an interface between decision making and religious consciousness, including the disciplined consciousness of theological inquiry.* Once we decide religion has some role to play in the conduct of capitalist enterprises, then the real task ahead is the reconstruction of the "sacred canopy" whose form and substance has yet to be articulated by any who entertain the acceptability of some degree of secularity. The dispensation of judgments concerning the secular tradeoffs may only have meaning in this context.[16]

Obviously there are many obstacles in the way, which have been summarized elsewhere, especially in the works of Peter Berger and Harvey Cox. My own Congregationalist bias suggests to me that the most fruitful avenues for effecting the interface of which I speak will be at the levels of personal conviction, human relations, and the establishment of other-world perspective in the mind of the real economic actors.[17] Krueger's introduction of the idea of personal transcendence into the business ethics dialogue is an important contribution, for it stretches the fabric of religious possibility beyond the outer-directed issues that usually preoccupy normative frameworks. What is less clear to me is how the business person can access this notion within the context of economic activity. If the two kingdoms are not separate, how will they be linked?

Thus my key challenge to Krueger and all normative theorists is to regard their task as incomplete—indeed, inadequate—until they have specifically provided entry points for theory to be applied to practice. For reasons stated above, I do not think the posing of macrodilemmas to be sufficiently viable entry. We might call this criterion the development of a moral viability test, the viability of theory to engage with practice in a way which does not pervert the meaning of the truths behind it.

The application of this test might even improve the legitimacy of theological mandates in the economic arena. At the risk of sounding more like a manager than an academic, I would suggest that viability is a terrific test of quality, even of theoretical quality. Frankly, we have seen almost every type of economic system defended at one time or another by a Christian normative approach, from the tolerance of megalomaniacal monarchy to totalitarian communism. This hat trick of academic theology seems to depend on two related conditions: (1) that the normative tests be strictly focused on intentions rather than results, and (2) that any claimed or predicted results not be hampered by ordinary criteria of proof such as a documentation of the relevant facts, or evidence that the theory is in any way capable of real application. (The chief enforcer of these conditions seems to me to be the professional language of extreme abstraction and generality in which most of these arguments are imbedded.) Thus we have witnessed contemporary theologians defend extreme forms of both communism and capitalism, and making theoretically robust arguments for both distributive and productive justice. All such theories, whether they are based on dogma, revelation, or logic, claim to be responsive to the word of God and the needs of the poor.

Clearly the typical test of theological quality—namely whether the grounding is right—is in need not of abandonment, but perhaps of some further refinement, if we are to bring theory to the point where it can legitimately be said to provide service to the world. The articulation of entry points to application would be a step in this direction.

Identifying the Devil

In order to construct viable entry points for theological reflection and theory, it is helpful to study contextual obstacles to the carrying out of this theoretical order. Different languages and density of argument are two obstacles already discussed above. Prof. Krueger has written of the obstacles of a sinful human nature. I would like to take into consideration several other external obstacles that seem endemic to the modern corporation's structure and the people working in it.

For the record, my own normative view of capitalism, which I first put forth in *Good Intentions Aside*,[18] is that there is inherently a possibility of basic compatibility between a Christian ethic of service and the ingredients of market success, but that such compatibility is not inevitable, nor does the basic ethic of market mechanisms on its own overcome questions of social justice. What capitalism does do is express a covenant between the public and the individual (and by extension the firm) that if someone provides true value creation, then he or she or it deserves a reward. The qualitative nature of value is not resolved by this framework, although the avoidance of harm is a logical precondition. The exact level of reward is not given precise criteria, but rather relies on a balance of market forces (consumer, capital, political and labor markets) that further the creation of enabling relationships. Despite its refusal to create a more refined set of principles, this basic covenant captures the balance of self-interest and other-oriented service of needs that seems to explain how good businesses get run and make profits. Thus it provides a model against which decision making might be tested. The covenant also describes the tenets of capitalism as a function of both rational and irrational impulses, thereby leaving open the possibility of vocation. It also provides a simple normative framework for placing such Christian duties as loving thy neighbor and enabling others as preconditions to the achievement of efficiency. It also sets forth the terms for the creation of legal restrictions and contractual guarantees: no ethical economic market system can survive without legal and universally enforced sanctions ensuring that value provision (and its concomitant avoidance of harm) will indeed be a systemic competitive advantage and thus rewarded. Polluters, free riders, privateers, and snake oil salespersons will be penalized.

Having said all this, I find the conditions for the moral viability of this covenant particularly daunting in today's corporation. We need to be aware of *a context of radical contradiction* that attends the execution of corporate goals in the marketplace. This is not simply the values contradictions that Daniel Bell so eloquently pointed out in *The Cultural Contradictions of Capitalism*,[19] but also contradictions of purpose, roles, tasks, and cultural norms—both inside the corporation and in the external conditions of worldwide markets that a corporation is likely to pursue. The phenomenon of globalization may exacerbate these conditions.

I would now like to consider several of these contradictions and see if there is not some viable entry point for applying Christian principles to the operation of business, including principles of productive justice or transformational ethics. As already noted, the functional tasks of the marketplace are now spread across the globe, but the cultural and political contexts in which these tasks are located differ widely and are often in contradiction. Say, for example, a telecommunications corporation wishes to set up production in Xanadu, a southeast Asian country somewhere east of India and west of Japan. Xanadu needs jobs. It would appear to be an act of productive justice and economic foresight to tap its relatively cheap labor supply.

Immediately, however, other ethical contradictions are posed. First of all, any increase in economic prosperity is likely to increase the political hold of Xanadu's oligarchy, a regime of insiders and cousins to the royal family which has regularly and brutally suppressed economic and religious freedom among the lower classes. It does so in part out of a belief in that the royal family is the incarnation of the divinity. The health of the family is the health of the nation. Building a new plant will draw transient workers to the area, and with them a new market for the forced prostitution of adolescents. The modest rise in gross wages in the village will invite other companies to aggressively compete for those dollars by marketing nonessential products. As Manager C tries to negotiate in Xanadu, taking into account the twenty-seven volumes of U.S. law regulating trade with Xanadu, the company's share price will happen to take a hit on stock market due to the sale of shares by a pension fund in Europe which is itself in hot water for manipulating its payouts. Time will be of the essence in getting the Xanadu project going in order to boost investor confidence. The fastest way to get local approval is to hire the king's first cousin as consultant. He in turn will get contracts quickly through the system but the construction workers will be from one ethnic group, none of them local. A private hit squad will need to be hired for reasons of personal security as the managers of the Xanadu project travel the country and try to carry out even simple banking activities such as meeting a payroll. The hit squad will exhibit the typical bullying habits of privatized security arrangements unfettered by a corrupt police force. Meanwhile, the prime minister issues a strict prohibition on the use of cellular phones by private individuals for reasons of state security, thereby killing a great market opportunity and also making it necessary for Company X managers to apply for special permits for their phones. When local workers use the phones, they will technically be subject to arrest, a practice which will be selectively enforced. Thus Company X will be inadvertently putting some workers at greater risk from political persecution. Once the plant is up and operating, loose environmental laws in Xanadu and local unconcern will inevitably lead to toxic emissions and water quality deterioration as the new telecommunications equipment is manufactured. In Company X's home country, two hundred employees (management and factory worker) will be downsized due to the closing of an older plant in the Midwest. And so on.

As Manager X's situation shows, one cannot operate in the global economy without encountering serious contradictions of law between countries; widespread differences of understanding about what such universal values as honesty or fairness really mean in practice; differing cultural and religious notions of the common good; and conflicting signals from investors, employees, and communities about what is the right way to do business. While the economic opportunities seem clear, the ethical opportunities are at best, very muddy. What Manager X most needs now is a support system, but as yet, no traditional religious, legal, political, or business institution has managed to effect a unification of purpose and values that crosses national and class boundaries to this extent. Individual partnerships on a limited level can secure a partial unification of values, but there has yet to be a creation of a global *community* to which economic actors might belong. There is no worldwide value support system for global capitalism that can secure the fundamental legal guarantees that are at the heart of the capitalistic covenant: free markets, value creation, avoidance and compensation of injury. Efforts to develop a universalized "international code" are underway, but even were they to agree on the words, they have no plan for overcoming the problems of local application or for gaining political/legal endorsement. Judging from the stalled efforts to create and enforce a unified set of rules for the European Community, success is a long way off.

Any normative justification of capitalism on theological or ethical grounds must provide a viable *way in* to these complex and intertwined issues. Even if the theology suggests a world of two separate kingdoms, there must be some engagement in the contradiction of forces that the real actors are facing.

The Xanadu scenario, despite its complexity of tasks, does not describe the economic actors. Were we to do so, we would have to confront not only the extreme contradictions of purpose, priorities, and worldview that envelope the multitasked business operation, but also the radical sense of personal contradiction that modern economic actors in large corporations have been seen to exhibit. While there appears to be a holistic trend in the United States toward personal integration of one's spiritual commitments, social roles, and work—a trend that is often characterized by the call to bring "one's whole self" to the task of management or by the psychological concept of the integrated personality—the reality is that most jobs in the modern globalized economy depend on the traditional fragmentation that threatens to render normal humans incapable of having an integrated sense of identity.

I have little theoretical argument with the idea that one should try to bring the whole self to one's work,[20] but the way work is fashioned for most people in corporations, dictates a suppression of the self at precisely that contact point where the self is most unique, as in moments of high emotion, radical restructuring of a problem, or stylistic expressionism. To achieve a dignity, stay serious about work, and create an impression of general trustworthiness, the corporate culture will reinforce a "safe" control over emotions, encourage a conformity of dress within the company's sartorial norms, and a suppress radical thinking in deference to the idea of corporate loyalty. Ironically, this kind of depersonalization is especially characteristic in larger corporations with a heavy emphasis on civility. Such anti-individualistic customs may seem trivial or to have only the desirable purpose of encouraging economic performance, but over time many managers have found that they have actually become who they had only pretended to be.

This dehumanization of the bureaucratic actor was noted long ago by Max Weber, who observed that bureaucracies must suppress all that is human and emotional for the sake of advancing their own survival. [21] At question here is whether any globalized ethic of productive justice could be enforced fairly without the creation of mega-bureaucratic institutions that in themselves invite the attendant evils of dehumanized and undemocratic institutions of power.

Globalism can exacerbate this suppression of the affections by imposing the stern discipline of multicultural tolerance, especially in an unknown culture. Our Manager X may be appalled at the treatment of minorities in Xanadu and uncomfortable with the hiring practices that are enforced by law, but will not entertain this outrage at the expense of the contract unless it can be disguised in corporatized arguments of enlightened self-interest: well, it would hurt us in the long run with our customers and shareholders if we were seen to be participating in Xanadu. Of course, this type of rationalization, repeated over time, is not only hypocritical, it is a subversion of the full range of emotions that drive Christian affection.

Another key problem is the integration of a manager's own multiple roles. Modernity increases fragmentation, specialization of tasks, and thus the roles people play. Society differentiates along multiple and sometimes conflicting activities: parenting, working, being a local citizen and member of a national party. All of which leaves the individual vulnerable to disintegration of a coherent personality and a society at odds with itself. Meanwhile there is simultaneously a condition of interdependence in the so-called global economy, a condition that is as inequitable to the participants as it seems inevitable to the growth of anybody's economic well-being. The postmodern mind is supposedly adept at entertaining multiple roles and meaning systems, but it would useful to the manager to find a clear distinction between what is a postmodern simultaneity and what is just plain old self-contradiction.

The corporation itself often reflects these contradictions in its own culture, especially when it is trying to be nurturing to individual needs. Global Manager X may be joining a family-friendly firm, but the global marketplace will keep him from seeing his family for weeks at a time. The company may sincerely wish to affirm its sense of obligation to the community, but it will do so only in a carefully endorsed fashion, sponsoring certain days or people to engage in volunteerism, but not releasing employees from overtime commitments so that they can engage as citizens in a local school board crisis or a legislative hearing on international fishing laws for their particular waters.

The list of contradictions could go on, but the basic areas of radical contradiction are clear: the contradiction of roles, customs, national and personal goals, and the gap between promised behavior and that which is inevitably altered by its dependence on multiple tasks for its execution.

Given these internal corporate contradictions, and absent any unifying external institutional support systems or mechanisms for personal integration such as those once offered by Calvin in a pre-management stage of capitalism, it is difficult to imagine how a theoretical explanation of a just economy—however sound from a theoretical standpoint—could overcome the obvious contradictions between a global ideal and nationalistic or individualistic limitations. One of the frequent solutions to this conundrum is the paradoxical slogan of our day, "Think globally, act locally." While the thought helps motivate me to pick up the litter on my own street, or seek to profile productive examples of corporate citizenship, neither this paradox, nor any passionate agreements that U.S. companies must participate in alleviating world poverty, will help me constructively interpret the fundamental dilemmas posed by any just economy teleology: When and how to balance local need with global need, or to determine who are legitimate "stakeholders" with a moral claim on a corporation's resources when many of these stakeholders have no legal power or representative authority. Why invest in Mexico over Guatemala? South Africa over Watts? Should a company globalize manufacturing if it contributes to the prosperity of a repressive government? On what grounds should the creation of jobs in a less developed country be a source of social or personal disintegration, as when travel in the global economy prevents executives from seeing their families or participating in the local life of a community for days or weeks at a time?

Postmodernism aside, the maintenance of the wide array of contextual paradoxes in the modern economy that nearly escape the bounds of rational consistency make a mockery of the neat rational constructions of most theological inquiry. Theological justifications fail to influence the preferences of the corporate stakeholders unless they develop viable entry points for the examination of these contradictory purposes and for personal and collective action.

Three Key Entry Points

With this in mind, it would be helpful to develop a short-list of essential conditions for the development of entry ways to theory. Three are offered here.

(1) *Know the flock.* We need not only a theory of the economy, but also a knowledge of the firm and of the economic culture driving local economies, which is then related back to the expression and application of theory. Henri Nouwen attributed his ability to influence the social debate and to provide individuals hope to the fact that he had exposed himself to the same vulnerabilities the lonely and the poor experienced. As he put it, "one of the reassuring things is to know that here is a person who has looked at it, faced it, but still stands straight." So too, the theologian of business ethics must walk in the shoes of the manager, in order to gain real experience of the fundamental tensions that threaten to separate the economic person from the sacred and the moral.

This is very difficult for many academicians and theologians. The very differences of worldview that can provide the basis for ethical insight also tend to separate preacher and executive. In my own work I have repeatedly observed that when asked to discuss a painful moral issue of business both the manager and the theologian will frequently choose layoffs as the topic. The manager will tell you how personally painful such situations are and why he or she had to implement the layoff despite the personal bleeding for the sake of larger corporate community. Any extension of the analysis will usually turn to the moral meaning behind *how* a layoff is conducted. In other words, the manager will complexify the context and simplify the moral lesson. The theologian will simplify the managerial context, drawing reference to the time a Christian manager bravely decided to keep a losing business going and let the rest of the firm carry the financial burden! It would be tempting to conclude that the two professionals were merely expressing different priorities. In fact they have annihilated each other's priorities and in so doing have cut off the possibility of communication. Why does this occur? For many theoreticians it is because the business person and the real world of complex management is not real, and thus not taken seriously enough for their own counter view to find a point of engagement. A language of abstraction completes the distancing.

Ironically, some clergy seeking to further their outreach to business groups overcompensate for the differences of language and professional culture by taking on the disguise of an economist. When they get into a business ethics forum, they propose global economic solutions and sure-fire corporate strategies for business success. Economic analysis is *not* their strong point, however, and rarely is such talk a fool-proof disguise. I recall one such discussion between theologians and business people where the theologians differed with each other over the optimal strategic direction for the firm, taking into consideration, of course, the global competition. Later one of the business people was found scratching his head in forlorn wonder. "I thought they were going to talk about *religion!*"

(2) *Beware the grandiose.* God is such a big idea that bigness tends to become contagious in theological discussions, thereby inviting the conventional pitfalls of a theory inaccessible to real people and real practices on a human scale. Professional language constructs its own professional fences, and like all fences, they keep things out but also keep things in. If relevance to the economic actor is an important

goal, the moral viability test demands that the dense, highly abstract formulation find a way of escaping its own fences. Even in the church's own economic endeavors, it's the concrete details that tend to get ignored in favor of the large idea (see the tragic examples of the New Era fund and the Pax World Fund) Of course there is a basic moral demand: that corporations contribute to the development of at least basic levels of material well-being consistent with requirements of human fulfillment. One could extend this call with infinite abstractions explaining the meaning of each of the concepts. None of these would provide the entry point for a transformational view of productive justice as well as a specific analysis of Xanadu's main characters and context.

(3) *Distinguish theological terms from marketplace terms.* Ironically, even as the conventional theological formulation remains embedded in deep abstraction and generalized views of the marketplace, the church is making ever new connections to the marketplace in order to be more responsive to the laity. A visit to today's megachurch or interfaith website may cause one to wonder whether one is encountering a social services agency, a media event, or a simple spin on niche marketing. It would be tempting to assume that the best way to provide entry point for theory into the commercial context would be to package it in commercial or therapeutic language, drawing on familiar advertising slogans and executive development programs for the depiction of religious meaning. The entry point, however, is not to be had by blurring all boundaries. Rather, it requires discovery of the legitimate, perceived intrusion of the transcendent in the marketplace.

Obviously the perception of this potential intrusion and the authority it exercises will differ according to religious belief, and that in itself should be a subject of inquiry in the theological analysis of globalism. But the point here is not to overcompensate the lack of connection between the theological view and the economic action by reducing all discussion to economically framed choices and vocabularies. An example would be the reduction of religious duty to the poor to a utilitarian argument about the potential market benefits of corporate social responsibility. A transformational theology should transform the language by which economic actors assess their purpose or evaluate their own sense of meaning in their activity. If one of the key problems of the postmodern manager is, as I have suggested, the disjointedness of roles and norms within one personality, then a clarification of realms is paramount. The Kingdom of Heaven may be too remote a concept for many, and so the creation of noncommercial paradigms for transformed mission and community will help executives reintegrate personality and faith into their lives.

To conclude, there is enormous need for the normative formulations about business purpose and responsibility to build into the theory the access points to practice. Doing so will necessitate a full understanding of the complexity of the global corporation, the complexity of clashing economic cultures, and the psychological complexity of the postmodern manager. For the achievement of global justice, these considerations must not only benefit others and the corporation, they must lead to the creation of new communities that transcend current tribal bounds, whether of a propertied or political nature. It would be my suspicion that, despite Alisdair McIntyre's disdain of the "secondary virtues" of cooperative processes such as teamwork,[22] the area of human relations in the marketplace will provide one of the key entry points for understanding the relevancy of the intrinsic truths of the Holy Spirit.

Another example of the ways in which attention to context and simplified language can effect theological relevancy is a perceptive discussion of exchange by Jon Gunnemann. In that discussion he offers a number of conceptual access points to understanding the nature of justice in exchange relationships.[23] Among the most interesting is the role of geographic and informational distance, examples of which illuminate fundamental inequities in the status quo of various exchange relationships. Gunnemann bases his analysis on careful observation of the players and their situations. In one notable example he shows how Robert Nozick's famous Wilt Chamberlain example, and its conclusions about the role of free exchange patterns and liberty, are based on an overly simplified description of the economic players and institutional structures governing the purchase of a basketball ticket. He shows that the real market is both more complex than Nozick's description and more subject to the phenomenon of distance. Gunnemann warns about the confusion of abstraction and reality at the end of his piece. Interestingly, he reports that he deliberately minimized the theological discussion out of a dissatisfaction with the way markets have been overly theologized and bolstered with metaphysical discussions of human nature: "My proposal is that we start more modestly and empirically."[24]

Were we to apply these three criteria to the essay under discussion, it would invite the author to go further, to undertake a specific contextualization of the ethical dilemmas raised, and to create new paths for the dialogue between theologian and economic actor to occur. Who knows? The dialogue itself might have a transcendent potential.

Chapter 4

In Response

David A. Krueger

I am grateful for Don Shriver's gracious and thoughtful response to my essay, for it communicates and makes transparent much about the person behind the words. Throughout his career, Shriver—social ethicist, churchman, committed Christian, teacher, senior executive, scholar, civic leader, compassionate neighbor—has demonstrated careful scholarship that aims both to be faithful to the Christian witness of scripture and the mission of the church, but also to be in careful dialogue with complicated and nuanced realities of social life that almost always deny simple analysis and solution.

Implicit within Shriver's questions, concerns, and disagreements with aspects of my argument is considerable backdrop of agreement and shared affirmations about Christian ethics, contemporary economic life, and about how one goes about trying to do Christian economic ethics (some of which Shriver makes explicit within his discussion). We both give assent to the need for transformation and to common Christian convictions about wealth, poverty, sin, and balances of institutional power within society that illustrate our shared inheritance of the perspectives from the Niebuhrs. Shriver's own professional commitments and writing, like mine, have included strong attention to the ethics of capitalist institutions, and more concretely to the difficult and sometimes more tedious and tenuous constructive task of trying to do ethical reflection and analysis of business corporations in ways that can be accessible to practitioners and not just "observer" ethicists within church or academy. In this sense, we both share a curiosity and commitment to consider how Christian ethics might provide not only critical judgment and caution (what Paul Tillich called "the Protestant Principle") but also constructive norms ("Catholic Substance") by which to assess the relative achievements of capitalist business organizations. But it would seem that the way this continuum from criticism to construction is balanced explains some of the contentions and different emphases (questions, topics, style). Every ethicist locates oneself somewhere along this continuum: Shriver, more toward Protestant critique, I more toward the constructive norms of Catholic substance, which I think is more appropriate to the conditioned affirmation of global capitalism. At the very least, therefore, Shriver's questions provide healthy suspicions and corrections to any project to construct a substantive ethical edifice—ever a fragile human quest given our susceptibility to error, self-deception and sin. At most, Shriver's criticisms may imply flaws so fundamental to my argument as to warrant its rejection. Yet, then, Shriver assumes the same constructive burden—to construct a more adequate edifice of economic institutional arrangements consistent with fundamental Christian convictions and norms—a project which he has not understood as the task of his essay.

Many of Shriver's concerns warrant response—for example, his desire for more attention to Christology and his desire that all Christians engage seriously with the narratives of scripture. Yet I do not address them here, for it seems obvious to me that scriptural motifs are implicit in basic presumptions about ethical arguments that are in the text. But I will respond to Shriver's deepest and most substantive concern about my argument—that I have neglected adequate attention to distributive justice in my discussion of the modern business corporation by making the concept of productive justice simply a matter of "contributive" justice. I do not think that is so, and I do not jettison distributive justice as a vital concept in Christian social ethics. It is essential to any modern discussion of social justice, deeply rooted in scripture's focus on compassion and justice, especially toward the poor, and developed over centuries within the theological ethics and the life and witness of Christian churches. But I do want to argue that the task of distributive justice is not one that is *primary* to business corporations as such, given their special social purpose to generate wealth for society. This is not to say that businesses should be unmindful of the distributive consequences of their activities on employees and others who have a financial stake in their operations. Indeed, to the extent that some inequalities of reward within an organization become so skewed as to generate substantial ill-will and lowered productivity among "rank-and-file" employees, they can cease to be fair or justifiable even on grounds of organizational effectiveness. In this sense, corporate efforts that attempt to distribute both financial success (e.g., profit-sharing, bonuses) as well as hardship (e.g., reductions in compensation) throughout the organization can be appropriate embodiments of productive justice.

The concept of productive justice, if adequately practiced within corporations, might well go a long way in correcting some inequality and injustice that requires government compensatory programs to begin with! For instance, racism and sexism, which generate discriminatory patterns and practices resulting in inequality of opportunity and rewards in the workplace, are clear contradictions to the vision of productive justice I have outlined above. Hence, while corporations do not have sufficient power or even the moral mandate to generate or guarantee some morally ideal distribution of wealth and income within society, they have some capacity, within the constraints dictated by their function, to prevent some distributive outcomes deemed unjust due to patterns of discrimination, such as racism and sexism in the workplace. In other words, many women and minorities would not become poor if they were not discriminated against in the workplace to begin with. Admittedly, I have largely left open the question of what mechanisms corporations should best utilize to combat such forms of discrimination from showing their face in the workplace (e.g., debates about affirmative action). In addition, corporations are not precluded from other auxiliary efforts to combat larger social trends that tend to create distributive outcomes that we might deem unjust, such as corporate philanthropy and employee community service. Such efforts by corporations are many and varied, especially within the tradition of volunteerism and public involvement that continues to function within the U.S. experience.

Rather, we should look primarily to other social institutions, especially government, for the task of distributive justice, through the various redistributive and compensatory activities embedded within its budgetary powers to tax and to spend—but this was not a primary task of my essay. Government can legitimately aim to affect a society's distribution of wealth and income, through patterns of taxation and income support (e.g., government entitlements) that transfer wealth from some to others. Government also can affect distributional patterns through its commitments to "infrastructure development." Public education is a notable example. As knowledge becomes even more valuable in the global economy, education will become even more decisive in separating the "haves" from the "have-nots." This suggests that public investments of various kinds will become even more vital strategically as society concerns itself with distributive justice. Yet this is a matter delegated primarily to government, not to the primary instruments of production in modern life.

Second, I would challenge some of Shriver's explicit, and often implicit, empirical assumptions about trends within corporations and the global economy, not necessarily to debunk his interpretations but to suggest that many of our empirical assessments of economic life are themselves open to question and contentious. For instance, should we be alarmed that the U.S.'s percentage of global trade or industrial output has shrunk dramatically since World War II? This is merely evidence that global economic output has grown dramatically, moving much of the rest of the world out of poverty with growth rates exceeding ours. Yet our economy, measured by overall output and by per capita levels, is much larger today than it was fifty years ago. While some transfers of wealth globally have "been bought at the expense of more than a few Americans," the net result has been overwhelmingly beneficial for most persons in our economy as well as for the economies of most other nations in the world. It may also be true that "Americans are not getting richer at the rate of a generation ago." Yet diminished growth rates from a previous period in our economic history also are not necessarily a sign of disease or decay, but may be a consequence of an economy's location within a larger process of economic development. I can think of no ethical defense from a Christian perspective for believing that the United States needs to remain the richest and most powerful nation in the world. Rather, our moral mandate is to ask how our nation's economic institutions, practices, wealth, and power can become the most effective possible vehicles for the alleviation of poverty worldwide. In this framework, the Christian's query "Who is my neighbor?" becomes radically globalized, making more tenuous presumptions of higher moral importance to the worker nearby in Cleveland than the worker far away in Calcutta.

Finally, though, I believe Shriver and I would hold the global capitalist system to similar ethical tests, grounded in the Christian faith as revealed through the biblical narratives. One central test is how an economy affects the poor (to use Shriver's words, a Hebrew ethic—affirmed by Christians—has "a low tolerance for neglecting the weak, the vulnerable, and marginal folk of their society"). Indeed, I affirm this as the primary litmus test for global capitalism and conditionally argue for it *as a means* to move substantial numbers of the world's poor out of poverty more effectively than any other available set of institutional arrangements. In this sense, wealth is better than poverty and more wealth is better than less wealth for most people on this planet; however, such wealth, although legally gained, must be radically conditioned by considerations of ecological sustainability as well as social justice. Dislocations of workers as well as continual, and often, unpredictable shifts in patterns of wealth and income are handmaidens of this global process, not to be ignored or morally discounted, but neither to be neatly and perfectly managed by mechanisms of governmental (or corporate) power and control. More realistically, social justice demands that government, as well as other social institutions, where available, attempt to provide social safety nets that "cushion the blow" and ease the difficult and painful transitions that many experience in a dynamic market economy. But finally, Shriver has aptly crystallized my economic vision as "the hope that grinding poverty may be eliminated from the human world and that business enterprise can be the instrument of this hope in ways that neither socialist nor liberal economies have been able to achieve in the twentieth century." He overstates his case by suggesting that my faith in capitalism formally matches liberation theologians' faith in socialism. For my affirmation of capitalism is conditioned both by its own performance (the pragmatic test of how well it succeeds or fails to satisfy fundamental ethical norms informed by our faith) and by deeper assumptions about the permanent reality of the human condition—with its twin propensities to demonstrate both goodness and sin.

Laura Nash's response raises equally challenging questions about my position, and indeed about the larger issues of how theological ethics makes judgments about economic systems and of whether and how it can say something meaningful and practical about business corporations, and the persons who work within them. Embedded within these concerns are fundamental questions about moral authority and language in the modern world. Nash is correct to criticize much of twentieth-century theological economic ethics (without citing persons or positions) for two related deficiencies, if not fundamental flaws: (1) its tendencies to justify or ground arguments and conclusions according to criteria of adequacy far removed from economic practice, and (2) its limited or flawed use of empirical evidence.

As an ethicist who has spent a good bit of professional time attempting to do ethics with business practitioners, and not only with academics, I share Nash's concern about the language of ethics. Academic ethicists and business practitioners tend to speak very different specialized languages—a fact replicated across fields and specializations in a highly complex modern world. This problem is not unique to theological business ethics. Economists do not always speak the language of business; and jurisprudence does not always speak the language of the trial. In some ways, indeed, the language of theological ethics may be no more specialized than the languages of business theory spoken among business academics or of business practice spoken within business corporations. The challenge is to become "bilingual" or even "multilingual"—to find ways to bridge the gaps of meaning and interest and to develop, as Nash argues, "entry points."

Lurking behind some of the differences between Nash's approach and my own are larger debates and contentions about epistemology and moral authority in a "postmodern" world characterized at least in part by diversity, ambiguity, specialization, and fragmentation of meaning and purpose. Nash has rightly labeled my project as an attempt to argue for universalizable moral principles applicable in a globalized market economy. In this sense, I reveal my affinities to traditions of natural law and locate myself in the "foundationalist," and not the "postmodern" camp of contemporary debates about truth and meaning in the world. Can we discern and practice general ethical norms across the diversity of systems of meaning and culture? Foundationalists say yes. Postmodernists say no—that diversity, difference, and fragmentation are so pervasive as to make this age-old quest vacuous. Nash's claims and arguments, on the other hand, reveal closer affinities to the postmodern position at certain points, not only by resisting generally my aim to construct universalizable norms, but also in her divergent descriptive and empirical views of the world. She would characterize my general interpretation of global trends toward greater democracy and more liberal markets as excessively optimistic and simplistic. She sees the reality of corporate decision making as much more nuanced, and indeed fraught with seemingly inevitable contradiction and clashes of values and interests than my own discussion has implied. She thinks that this global economy is so fraught with contradiction as to render the very quest for universalizable systems of ethical values and norms in business (and society) to be at the very least highly difficult to embody in business practice, if not suspect at a deeper level of intellectual sustainability. In sum, some of our differences illustrate much deeper fault lines that have become defining debates of our era—and matters that cannot be adequately resolved in our discussion here.

Nevertheless, I will try to respond to this challenge by reiterating and clarifying some of my claims. Nash is right to remind us that the post-cold war world is by no means free from conflict, vulnerabilities, and challenges. Transitions from centrally-planned and other forms of statist economies and from totalitarian and other nondemocratic political regimes are by no means everywhere smooth, peaceful, and unblemished. Democratic virtues, including respect for law, and the responsible use of liberty, and its supporting institutional safeguards do not spring up *ex nihilo* from a totalitarian past— authoritarian impulses will continue to show their face in this political transition. Likewise, we should not assume that well-functioning competitive markets and systems of private property protected by law should sprout and flourish, untarnished by corruption, cartelization, and even rapid bursts of inequality in income and wealth. Nevertheless, recent events exhibit more than the mere collapse of communism. Concurrent, widespread global trends toward democratic government and competitive, liberal market economies are also irrefutable, albeit not yet clearly universal. Hence, my claims are not merely aspirational, but also sustained by a growing body of factual evidence.

Likewise, Nash's hypothetical portrayal of Company X seeking to do business in Xanadu is an apt illustration of the kinds of moral complexities and competing interests that corporations and their decision makers can find as they do business in a diverse, cross-cultural global economy. No doubt, this complexity generates moral ambiguity in the face of sometimes conflicting interests, moral goods and harms that can cause moral confusion to the point of seemingly inextricable moral morass. Yet the reality of moral complexity, ambiguity, conflict, and sometimes seeming confusion is not sufficient evidence to conclude that the global economy is so morally confused and chaotic to prevent its participants and observers from seeking overarching moral norms and guidelines that can be widely shared and promulgated across cultures. For instance, while bribery and corruption may yet be common practice in many parts of the global economy, no society enshrines them in law or publicly defends them as morally superior to their absence. Nor, for example, are infringements and violations of property rights so widespread as to counteract larger global trends toward the standardization of rules and regulations governing fair trade (e.g., through the widening scope of the World Trade Organization). Nor are global corporations unable to articulate, promulgate, and strive to embody in practice throughout their organization, ethical guidelines, standards, rules, and so forth, that can aid their people in resolving the very kinds of difficult moral dilemmas that Nash poses in her hypothetical scenarios in Xanadu. Again, my point is not to deny the reality of moral perplexity, ambiguity, tradeoffs, and indeed even conflict among values and interests in business practice that Nash so ably portrays. It is only to suggest that she has not provided sufficient evidence to conclude that "contradiction" and moral fragmentation are the predominant features of the contemporary global economy, or that, if it were, the clarification of guiding principles to sort through the mess would be useless.

Finally, therefore, I am left to wonder how Nash would evaluate the substantive components of my theory of productive justice. (How would it fare by her "moral viability test"?) Would she think criteria such as products that do not harm users and society, and long-term environmental sustainability are intelligible, defensible, and practical for corporations and their managers? Can they be effective factors (among many) that can actually motivate and shape the policies, practices, and behaviors of firms? Or must they be rejected in favor of some other plausible alternatives? My own reading of Nash's distinguished work in the field of business ethics suggests that her own fundamental moral commitments are not dissimilar from my own presented here.

In regard to her position, and Shriver's, and all the serious people their views represent, my concluding observation is that we can talk. We share more than we differ, and that is what I think a transformative theological ethic focused on productive justice illumines.

Notes

Notes to Chapter 1

1. The exceptions to this view are few and scattered. Roman Catholic theology could claim the North American voice of John A. Ryan, with his comprehensive ethical evaluation of U.S. capitalism, grounded in a Thomistic natural law. The World Council of Church's early motif of "the responsible society" provided the foundation for constructive moral judgments until sea changes in ecumenical social thought shifted toward liberationist perspectives in the 1960s and 1970s, only now being re-evaluated by some such as Ronald Preston (1991, 1994). Minority voices in the U.S. emerged later in the century, such as Robert Benne (1981) and Kuhn and Shriver (1991) among Protestants, and Michael Novak (1982, 1993), among Roman Catholics. But these views had been frozen out of most ecumenical discussions until more recently. Others have now emerged as well, cf. Atherton (1992), Stackhouse (1987, 1995), Krueger (1994), as well as some evangelical voices, cf. Chewning, Eby, and Roels (1990). See also the recent anthology edited by Stackhouse, McCann, and Roels (1995), the most comprehensive resource available in the field of religion and economic life.

2. This matter is carefully discussed also in Lake Lambert, "Called to Business: Corporate Stewardship as Vocation," Ph.D. dissertation, Princeton Theological Seminary, 1997.

3. I have developed these categories more fully in "Can Christian Ethics Inform Business Practice? A Typological Road Map and Criteria of Adequacy for an Ethic of Capitalism," in Samuel M. Natale and Brian M. Rothschild (editors), *Work Values: Education, Organization, and Religious Concerns* (Amsterdam: Rodopi, 1994), 53–71. In his Maurice Lectures of 1977, Ronald Preston also used Niebuhr's typology to categorize some Christian responses to capitalism (1979).

4. The independent nonprofit Investor Responsibility Research Center (IRRC) in Washington D.C. has provided leadership in cataloguing and analyzing these efforts, providing useful materials for both corporate and noncorporate members.

5. The Interfaith Center for Corporate Responsibility (ICCR) in New York City, sponsored by dozens of member denominations and religious orders, has served as the primary catalyst and coordinator for such efforts within the mainline U.S. religious community.

Notes to Chapter 2

1. Glen H. Stassen, Diane M. Yeager, and John Howard Yoder, *Authentic Transformation: A New Vision of Christ and Culture* (Nashville: Abingdon Press, 1996).

2. Helmut Reihlen, "The Rich and Poor Worlds: Is There a Way to Global Justice? The Example of Western Europe and Its Eastern Neighbors" (typescript of the third Bonhoeffer Lectures, given at Union Theological Seminary in New York on October 1, 1996), 10. Dr. Reihlen, a business executive, is president of the German Institute for Standardization and lay chairman of the Berlin-Brandenburg Synod of the Evangelical Church in Germany.

3. As quoted by Laurent A. Parks Deloz, et al., in *Common Fire: Lives of Commitment in a Complex World* (Boston: Beacon Press, 1996), 65, from Marstin, *Beyond Our Tribal Gods* (Maryknoll, NY: Orbis Books, 1979), 37.

4. *The New York Times* (September 28, 1996).

Notes to Chapter 3

1. Percival Wiksell, quoted in *The Value of Simplicity*, ed. Mary Minerva Barrows (Boston: H. M. Caldwell Company, 1905), 114. From Professor Ralph Potter's bibliography "The Rise and Fall of the Simple Life," Harvard Divinity School, Fall 1993.

2. Pam Woodall, "The hitchhiker's guide to cybernomics," *The Economist, A Survey of the World Economy* (September 28, 1996): 4.

3. I would refer the reader to one grave and one trivial indication that any celebration of communism's permanent death is probably premature: (1) Alexander Ledbed, and (2) a sign that recently appeared in a Harvard Square shop window which read, "Celebrate the fall of the U.S.S.R. Now *real* communism can have its birth!!"

4. Samuel P. Huntington, *The Clash of Civilizations and the Remaking of World Order* (New York: Simon & Schuster, 1996).

5. Ibid., 67.

6. See, e.g., Colin Campbell, *The Romantic Ethic and the Spirit of Modern Consumerism* (Oxford: Basil Blackwell, 1987).

7. Fernand Braudel, *Afterthought on Material Civilization and Capitalism*, trans. Patricia Ranum (Baltimore: The Johns Hopkins University Press, 1979); see esp. Part III, "Capitalism and Dividing Up the World."

8. Adolf A. Berle, Jr., *The 20th Century Capitalist Revolution* (New York: Harcourt, Brace and Co., 1954), 183.

9. Tom Donaldson and Thomas Dunfee, "Integrative Social Contracts Theory: A Communitarian Conception of Economic Ethics," *Economics and Philosophy* 11/1 (1995): 85–112.

10. R. H. Tawney, *Religion and the Rise of Capitalism* (New York: Mentor Publishers, 1937), 226.

11. Michael Novak, "Can a Christian Work for a Corporation?", *The Judeo-Christian Vision and the Modern Corporation*, ed. Oliver Williams and

John Houck (Notre Dame, IN: University of Notre Dame Press, 1982), 175.

12. Richard Rorty, "Cosmopolitanism without Emancipation," in *Modernity and Identity,* ed. Scott Lash and Jonathan Friedman (Oxford: Blackwell, 1992), 65.

13. Ronald M. Green, *Religion and Moral Reason: A New Method for Comparative Study* (New York: Oxford University Press, 1988), 3.

14. Oliver Williams' important field-based study of these effects was not available in time for this publication.

15. Joseph Biancala, "Defining the Proper Corporate Constituency: Asking the Wrong Question," *University of Cincinnati Law Review* 59/2 (1990): 434–36.

16. For an excellent discussion of the ironic difficulties of constructing such a view without disguise, see Timothy L. Fort, "Religious Belief, Corporate Leadership, and Business Ethics," *American Business Law Journal* 33 (1966): 451–71.

17. For an example of the latter world view, see the many interviews in my book, *Believers in Business* (Nashville: Thomas Nelson Publishers, 1994).

18. Laura L. Nash, *Good Intentions Aside: A Manager's Guide to Resolving Ethical Problems* (Boston: Harvard Business School Press, 1993).

19. Daniel Bell, *The Cultural Contradictions of Capitalism* (New York: Basic Books, Inc., 1976).

20. For a summary of the issues, see Laura L. Nash, "The Virtual Job," *Wilson Quarterly* (Autumn 1994): 72–81.

21. Max Weber, *Essays in Sociology* (New York: Oxford University Press, 1958), chapter VIII.

22. Alisdair MacIntyre, *A Short History of Ethics* (New York: Collier Books, 1966).

23. Jon P. Gunnemann, "Capitalism and Commutative Justice," *The Annual of the Society of Christian Ethics* (1985): 101–23.

24. Ibid, 122.

Contributors

David A. Krueger, previously Executive Director of the Center for Ethics and Corporate Policy in Chicago, currently holds the Charles E. Spahr Chair in Managerial and Corporate Ethics at Baldwin-Wallace College. He is the author of *Keeping the Faith at Work: The Christian in the Workplace* (Abingdon, 1994) and of many scholarly articles and Lutheran church documents.

Donald W. Shriver, Jr. is President of the Faculty and William E. Dodge Professor of Applied Christianity, *Emeritus*, at Union Theological Seminary in New York. He is the author of many volumes on ethics and economic life, from his earliest *Spindles and Spires*, a study on religion and labor in a southern mill town, to his recent *Beyond Success: Corporations and their Critics in the 1990s*, with James W. Kuhn (Oxford, 1991).

Laura L. Nash, previously on the faculty of the Harvard Business School, is now a member of the faculty at the Institute for the Study of Economic Culture at Boston University. She is known for her field-based studies of how ethics works in business, and is the author of *Good Intentions Aside* (Harvard Business School Press, 1993) and *Believers in Business* (Thomas Nelson, 1994).

Max L. Stackhouse is Professor of Christian Ethics and Director of the Project on Public Theology at Princeton Theological Seminary. He is the author of *Public Theology and Political Economy* (University Press of America, 1991), *Creeds, Society and Human Rights* (Eerdmans, 1984; Parthenon, 1996), *Christian Social Ethics in a Global Era* (with Peter L. Berger, Dennis P. McCann, and M. Douglas Meeks; Abingdon, 1995), and the primary editor of *On Moral Business* (Eerdmans, 1995).